THE WAY
OF LIFE

THE WAY OF LIFE

A Fresh Look at the Glorious
Gospel of Jesus Christ

**BY SPURGEON, TALMAGE, MOODY,
MILLS, CHAPMAN, AND MCNEILL**

We enjoy hearing from our readers. Please contact us at www.anekopress.com/questions-comments with any questions, comments, or suggestions.

Cover Designer: Jonathan Lewis

Editors: Paul Miller, J. Martin

Aneko Press

www.anekopress.com

Aneko Press, Life Sentence Publishing, and our logos are trademarks of

Life Sentence Publishing, Inc.

203 E. Birch Street

P.O. Box 652

Abbotsford, WI 54405

RELIGION / Christian Living / Inspirational

Paperback ISBN: 979-8-88936-112-1

eBook ISBN: 979-8-88936-113-8

10 9 8 7 6 5 4 3 2

Available where books are sold

CONTENTS

Chapter 1

ALL THINGS ARE READY: COME

By Charles H. Spurgeon

A certain man made a great supper, and bade many; and sent his servant at supper time to say to them that were bidden, Come; for all things are now ready. And they all with one consent began to make excuse. The first said unto him, I have bought a piece of ground, and I must needs go and see it. I pray thee have me excused. And another said, I have bought five yoke of oxen, and I go to prove them. I pray thee have me excused. And another said, I have married a wife, and therefore I cannot come. So that servant came and showed his lord these things. Then the master of the house being angry said to his servant, Go out quickly into the streets and lanes of the city, and bring in hither the poor, and the maimed, and the halt,

and the blind. And the servant said, Lord, it is
done as thou hast commanded, and yet there
is room. And the lord said unto the servant, Go
out into the highways and hedges, and compel
them to come in, that my house may be filled.
For I say unto you that none of those men
which were bidden shall taste of my supper.
– Luke 14:16-24

*C*ome; for all things are now ready. This invitation
was first of all made to the Jews, but it seems to me
to be especially appropriate to ourselves. It is later in the
day than when the Lord was first here, and therefore the
supper time is evidently closer at hand. The shadows
lengthen, and the sun of the present age is nearing its
setting. Since the Lord first sent forth His servants at
supper time, its day has been shortened by nearly two
thousand years. The fullness of time for the marriage
supper of the Lamb must quickly arrive.

If all things could be said to be ready even in our
Savior's day, we may say it with still greater emphasis
now; for when Jesus delivered this parable, the Holy
Spirit was not yet poured out on men. Now, however,
Pentecost has passed, and the Spirit of God abides with
us to accompany the Word and to fill it with power and
bless our souls as we feed upon the truth. Very certainly,
then, at this time all things are now ready, and the supper
awaits the guests. I ask you not to begin to make excuses,
but be prepared to follow us when we call you to come,

to go with us when we seek to bring you in, or at least to yield to our pleadings when, with all the sacred intensity of love, we would compel you to come in.

INVITATION AND ARGUMENT

There are two things clearly in the text, and these have a close relation to one another. There is a plain invitation: *Come*, and then a forcible argument: *for all things are ready*. The argument is brought from the divine preparations, gathered from among the excellent food of the royal feast. *My oxen and my fatlings are killed, and all things are ready* (Matthew 22:4). Come to the supper. The readiness

> The Lord has great forethought, and every little point of detail is well arranged.

of everything on God's part is the reason why people should come and partake of His grace. That is the point upon which we will dwell at this time. The readiness of the feast of mercy is the reason why people should come to it at once.

GOD IS NEVER LATE

It is God's nature to have all things ready, whether for His guests or His creatures. You never find Him to be behind or late in anything. When the guests come, there is not a scramble to get the table arranged and the food prepared, but the Lord has great forethought, and every little point of detail is well arranged. *All things are now ready.*

It was so in creation. God did not create a single blade of grass upon the face of the earth until the soil and the atmosphere had been prepared for it, and until the beneficent sun had learned to look down upon the earth. Imagine vegetation without a sun or without the changing of day and night. However, the air was full of light, the firmament upheld the clouds, and the dry land appeared from out of the sea – and then all things were ready for herb and plant and tree.

Nor did God prepare one single creature that has life, nor bird that flies in the midst of the sky, nor fish that swims the seas, nor beast that moves on the dry land until He had prepared its habitat and made ready its appointed food. There were no cattle before there were meadows for their grazing, no birds until there were trees for their nests, and not even a creeping insect until its portion of food had been provided. No creature had to hungrily wait while its food was growing. All things were ready – first for vegetation, and then afterward for animal life.

As for Adam, when God came to make him as His last and noblest work of creation, all things were ready. The garden was laid out upon the banks of flowing streams, and it was planted with all kinds of trees. The fruits were ripe for his nourishment, and the flowers were in bloom for his delight. He did not come to an unfurnished house, but he entered upon a home that his Father had made pleasant and delightful for his dwelling. The world was first made ready, and then the man who was to govern that world was placed in it. "All things are ready," the Lord seems to say. "Spring up, O herb yielding seed. All things are ready. Come forth, you deer of the fields. All things are ready. Come forth, O man, made in My own image!"

GOD'S THOUGHTS GO BEFORE MEN'S COMINGS

The fact that all things are ready in the great gospel supper teaches us that God's thoughts go before men's arrival. *Come; for all things are now ready.* He did not say, "If you come, all things will be ready," but "They are ready; therefore, come." Grace is first, and man at his best follows its footsteps. Long before we ever thought of God, He thought of us. Yes, before we had a being, and before time itself began, in the heart of the Eternal, there were thoughts of love toward those for whom

> Long before we ever thought of God, He thought of us.

the table of His mercy is now spread. He had planned and arranged everything in His majestic mind from of old. He had indeed foreknown and predestined all the provisions and all the guests of His supper. All things were settled in His eternal covenant and purpose before the earth ever was.

Never think, oh, sinner, that you can outdo the love of God. It is at the end of the race before you are at the beginning. God has completed before you have begun. His thoughts are before ours, and so are His acts, for He does not say, "All things are planned and arranged," but *All things are now ready.* Jesus, the great sacrifice, is slain. The fountain for our cleansing is filled with blood. The Holy Spirit has been given. The Word by which we are to be instructed is in our hands. The light that will illuminate that sacred page is promised to us through the Holy Spirit.

Things promised should encourage us to come to Christ, but things already given should be irresistible attractions. All things are already completed by the sacred Trinity before we come to cry for mercy. This should make us very hopeful and eager as we approach the Lord. Come, sinner, come at once. This should encourage you since all that God has to do in your salvation has already been done before you had one thought of Him or turned one foot in His direction. All are welcome! Things are ready. Come!

This also proves how welcome those are who come. If you are invited to see a friend, and when you reach the place, you find the door closed and locked, and after knocking many times no one answers because there is no one at home, you suppose that there has been some mistake or that the invitation was not a sincere one. Even if your host would come to the door and let you in, but would clearly be embarrassed because there is no meal provided and he has made no arrangements for your rest at night, you soon realize it, and like a wise man, you quickly leave, for if you had been welcome, things would have been prepared for you. But oh, poor soul, if you come to God, all things are ready for your delight.

> Spread for thee the festal board,
> With his richest dainties stored.[1]

---

1   This is from a hymn by Thomas Haweis (1734-1820) that begins with "From the cross uplifted high."

The couch of rest and quietness is prepared for you. All things are ready. How freely Jehovah welcomes you! How genuine is the invitation! How sincere is the desire that you would come to feast with Him!

I GO TO PREPARE A PLACE FOR YOU

One of these days, it may be that you and I will either have grown very old, or else disease will lay hold upon us, and we will lie upon the sickbed watching and waiting for our Master's coming. Then there will suddenly appear a messenger from Him who will bring us this word: "All things are ready. Come to the supper." Then, closing our eyes on earth, we will open them in heaven and see what He has done who so graciously said, *I go to prepare a place for you. And if I go to prepare a place for you, I will come again and receive you unto myself, that where I am, there ye may be also* (John 14:2-3). It will be a joyous moment when we will hear the call, "All things are ready. Leave your house of clay, your farm, your merchandise, and even her who lies in your arms, for the marriage of the Lamb has come, and you must be there. Therefore, *Rise up, my love, my fair one, and come away. For lo, the winter is past . . . ; the time of the singing of birds is come* for you [Song of Solomon 2:10-12]. All things are ready. Come!"

The perfect readiness of the feast of divine mercy is evidently intended to be a strong argument with sinners why they should come at once. Therefore, I now address myself to the sinner.

Soul, do you desire eternal life? Is there within your spirit a hungering and a thirsting after such things that may satisfy your spirit and make you live forever? Then listen while the Master's servant gives you the invitation. *Come; for all things are now ready* – all; not some, but all. There is nothing that you can need between here and heaven that is not provided in Jesus Christ, in His person and in His work. All things are ready: life for your death, forgiveness for your sin, cleansing for your filth, clothing for your nakedness, joy for your sorrow, and strength for your weakness. Yes, more than all that you can ever need is stored up in the boundless nature and work of Christ.

The great Householder Himself has provided everything needed for the feast.

You must not say, "I cannot come because I do not have this, or do not have that." Are you to prepare the feast? Are you to provide anything? Do you need to supply even so much as the salt or the water? You do not know your true condition or you would not dream of such a thing. The great Householder Himself has provided everything needed for the feast. You have nothing to do with providing it, but are to simply partake of it. If you lack, come and take what you lack.

The greater your need, the greater reason why you should come where all things that you can possibly need will be at once supplied. If you are so needy that you have nothing good at all about you, all things are ready. What would you provide more when God has provided all things? It would be *superfluity of naughtiness* (James 1:21) if you were to think of adding to His *all things.* You would be presumptuously competing with the provisions of the great King, and this He will not tolerate. All that you need – I can only repeat the words – between the gates of hell, where you now lie, and the gates of heaven, to which grace will bring you if you believe – all is provided and prepared in Jesus Christ the Savior.

READY

All things are now ready. Dwell on that word *ready.* The oxen and the fatlings were killed. What is more, they were prepared to be eaten, they were ready to be feasted on, and they were ready on the table. It is something when the king gives orders for the slaughter of so many bullocks for the feast, but the feast is not ready then; and when the animals are slaughtered, and they are stripped and hung up ready for the fire, there is something done, but they are not ready. When the meat is served hot and steaming upon the table, and all that is wanted is brought forth and laid in proper order for the banquet, it is then that all things are ready – and this is the case now.

At this very moment, you will find the feast to be in the best possible condition. It was never better and never can be better than it is now. All things are ready and are in the exact condition that you need them to be. They are in just such a condition that will be best for your soul's comfort and enjoyment. All things are ready. Nothing needs to be further developed or sweetened. Everything is at the best that eternal love can make it.

NOW!

Notice the word "now." *All things are now ready.* They are ready right now, at this moment. As you know, at feasts, the good housewife is often troubled if the guests come late. She would be sorry if they came half an hour too soon, but half an hour too late spoils everything. In what a state of frustration and worry she is if, when all things are now ready, her friends have still not arrived. If the food is left in the oven awhile longer, it does not seem to be now ready, but is more than ready, and even spoiled.

So the Great Householder emphasizes that all things are *now* ready; therefore, come at once. He does not say that if you will wait another seven years, all things will then be ready. God desires that you, long before that space of time, may have got beyond the needs of persuasion by having become a taster of the feast. Instead, He does say that things are all ready, right now. Right now, when your heart is so heavy, your mind is so careless, and your spirit is so wandering, all things are ready *now*, even though you have never thought of these things before. Even though your sins are as many as the stars of heaven and your soul trembles under a dreadful foreboding of coming judgment, yet *all things are now ready.*

If they are ready *now*, then the argument is for you to come *now*. While the Spirit lingers and still strives with people, while mercy's gates still stand wide open so that *whosoever will* may come (Revelation 22:17), while life and health and reason are still spared to you, and while the ministering voice that urges you to come can still be heard, come now; come at once! Now that all things are ready, delay is as unreasonable as it is wicked.

Reader, if you do not come to Christ, you will perish; but you never will be able to say that you were not called to come.

YOU DO NOT NEED TO WAIT UNTIL YOU ARE READY

This text gets rid of a great deal of talk about the sinner's readiness or unreadiness because if the reason why a sinner is to come is because all things are ready, then it is useless for him to say, "But I am not ready." It is clear that all the readiness required on man's part is a willingness to come and receive the blessing that God has provided. Where the Lord has been pleased to touch the will so that man has a desire toward Christ, where the heart really hungers and thirsts after righteousness – that is all the readiness needed. All the preparation He requires is that (1) you feel your need of Him (and He gives you that), and that in feeling your need of Him, (2) you are willing to come to Him.

All the readiness required is a willingness to come and receive the blessing that God has provided.

Willingness to come is everything. A readiness to believe in Jesus, a willingness to cast your soul on Him, and a preparedness to accept Him just as He is because you feel that He is just the Savior that you need – that is all. There is no other readiness needed, and there

11

could have been none in the case of those who were poor and blind and halt and maimed (Luke 14:21), yet who came to the feast. The text does not say, "You are ready; therefore come." That is a legal way of putting the gospel. Instead, it says, *"All things are now ready. The gospel is ready. Therefore, you are to come."*

WHY DO YOU DELAY?

Now notice that the unreadiness of those who were called arose because of their possessions and their duties. One person would not come because he had bought a piece of land. What a large hill Satan mounds up between the soul and the Savior! With what worldly possessions and good deeds he builds an earthwork of huge dimensions between the sinner and his Lord! Some gentlemen have too many acres to ever come to Christ. They think too much of the world to think much of Him. Many people have too many fields of good works in which there are growing crops in which they pride themselves, and these cause them to feel that they are people of great importance. Many people cannot come to Christ for all things because they have so much already. Others could not come because they had so much to do, and could do it well. One man had bought five yoke of oxen, and he was going to test them. He was a strong man quite able to plow, and the reason why he did not come was because he had so much ability.

Thousands of people are kept away from grace by what they have and by what they can do. Emptiness is a much better qualification for a feast than fullness.

How often does it happen that poverty and inability even help to lead the soul to Christ! When a person thinks he is rich, he will not come to the Savior. When a person dreams that he is able to repent at any time and believe and to do everything for himself that is needed, he is not likely to come to Christ, and certainly not rest in Christ by a simple faith.

It is not what they do not have, but what they have, that keeps many from Christ. Sinful self is a devil, but righteous self is seven devils. The person who feels himself guilty may be kept away by his guilt for awhile, but the person who is self-righteous will never come. Until the Lord has taken his pride away from him, he will still refuse the feast of free grace. The possession of abilities and honors and riches keeps people from coming to the Redeemer.

On the other hand, personal condition does not mean that one is unfit to come to Christ, for the sad condition of those who became guests did not exclude them from the supper. Some were poor and were undoubtedly wretched and ragged. They did not have a penny to bless themselves with, as we say. Their garments were tattered, perhaps worse. They were filthy and were not fit to be near respectable people. They would certainly be no credit to my Lord's table, but those who went to bring them in did not search their pockets or look at their coats, but they simply brought them in. They were poor, but the messengers were told to bring in the poor, and therefore they brought them. Their poverty did not prevent them from being ready.

Oh, poor soul, if you are poor literally, or poor inherently, neither sort of poverty can cause you to be unfit for divine mercy.

Another group of people were maimed. One had lost a nose, and another had lost an arm. So, poor soul, no matter how Satan may have torn and cut you, and no matter into what condition he may have brought you so that you feel ashamed to live – you may come to the table of grace just as you are. Moral disfigurements are soon rectified when Jesus takes you in hand. Come to Him, no matter how sadly you are disfigured by sin.

There were others who were halt, or lame. That is, their leg was of no use to them, and they could not come unless they had a crutch to lean upon. Nevertheless, there was no reason why they were not welcome. If you find it difficult to believe, it is no reason why you should not come and receive the marvelous pardon that Jesus Christ is ready to bestow upon you. If you are lame with doubting and mistrusting, nevertheless come and say, *Lord, I believe; help thou mine unbelief* (Mark 9:24).

Others were blind, but a blind man can come if a messenger brings him. All that was needed was a willingness to be led by the hand in the right direction. You who cannot fully understand the gospel, who are puzzled and confused, give your hand to Jesus and be willing to be led by Him. Be willing to believe what you cannot understand and to grasp in confidence that which you are not yet able to measure with your understanding.

Here comes a poor man who has had nothing to eat for the last forty-eight hours. Look at his eager delight at the sight of the food! If you want somebody to eat heartily and joyfully, is not he the man? See how he takes it in! It is wonderful how the provisions disappear before him! Now here is a poor woman who has been picked up by the wayside, weak for lack of bread. She has hardly any life in her, but see how she begins to open her eyes at the first morsel that

> The greatness of your need is your suitableness for coming to Christ.

is placed before her! See what delight there is in her every expression as she finds herself placed at a table so richly loaded!

Yes, the poorer, the more hungry, and the more destitute the guests, the more honor is due to the king who feeds such paupers and receives such vagrants to his table. Hear how they shout the king's praises when they are filled with his food! They will never be done thanking him.

If I address a soul that is very needy, very weak, and very despairing, you are a proper guest for my Master because you have such a fine appetite for His generous table of love. The greatness of your need is your suitableness for coming to Christ, and if you want to know how to come, come just as you are. Do not wait to improve yourself one single bit. Come as you are.

HOW CAN I COME TO CHRIST?

You say, "I hear that if I come to Christ, I will be saved; but how can I come to Him? What do you mean by 'coming to Jesus'?" Well, our reply is plain and clear: it is to trust Christ, to depend upon Him, to believe

Him, and to rely upon Him. You ask, "But how can I come to Christ? In what way would you recommend me to come?" The answer is: the very best way to come to Christ is to come with all your needs about you.

Suppose a physician would come to town and let it be known that what he wants is not to make money, but to cure people out of motives of pure benevolence, without charging any fees, and that the poorest will be welcomed and the most diseased will be best received. Well, here is a person who has cut his finger. Will the doctor rush to take care of him? Here comes another free-of-charge patient who has a wart on his hand. There is nothing outstanding about curing cut fingers and warts, and the physician is by no means excited about the work.

The very best way to come to Christ is with all your needs about you.

However, here is a poor, hopeless body who has been given up by all the other doctors, a patient who is so bad that he lies at death's door. He has such a complication of diseases that he could hardly tell what diseases he has not suffered from, but certainly his condition is terrible enough to make it appear hopeless. He seems to be a living wonder of disease. That is the man who may come boldly to the physician and expect his immediate attention and his best consideration.

Now, doctor, if you can cure this man, he will be a credit to you. This man exactly answers to your description of those whom you came to help. You say that you only want patients who will give you an opportunity to display your skill. Here is a fine object for your compassion. His lungs, heart, feet, eyes, ears, and head are all bad. He is bad all over. If you want an opportunity to show your skill, here is the man.

Jesus, my Lord and Master, is the Great Physician of souls, and He heals them on just such terms as I have mentioned. Are you a weary sinner? Are you a deeply sin-sick soul? Are you a man or woman who is completely bad? Come along, my friend. You are just in the right condition to come to Jesus Christ. "Come just as you are" is the best way to come.

"What?" someone says. "Do you mean it – that I, a hard-hearted, unrepentant wretch, am called to come at once and believe in Jesus Christ for everlasting life?" Yes, I mean just that. I do not mean to send you around to that shop for repentance, and to the other shop for feeling, and to a third store for a tender heart, and then eventually direct you to call on Christ for a few odds and ends. No, no – but come to Christ for everything.

> Come, ye needy, come and welcome,
>   God's free bounty glorify;
> True belief and true repentance,
>   Every grace that brings you nigh,
> Without money,
>   Come to Jesus Christ and buy.[2]

I heard of a shop some time ago in a country town where they sold everything, and the man said that he did not believe that there was anything a human being wanted that he could not furnish him with from head to toe.

---

2   This is from a hymn by Joseph Hart (1712-1768) that begins with "Come, ye sinners, poor and wretched."

Well, I do not know whether that promise would have been carried out to the letter if it had been tried, but I know it is so with Jesus Christ. He can supply you with all you need, for *Christ is all* (Colossians 3:11). There is not a need your soul can possibly have that the Lord Jesus Christ cannot supply, and the very best way to come is to come to Him for everything.

Trust Jesus Christ – that is all – just as you are, with all your inabilities and unreadiness. Take what God has made ready for you: the precious blood to cleanse you, a robe of righteousness to cover you, and eternal joy to be your portion. Receive the grace of God in Christ Jesus, and receive it now. May God grant that you will, for Jesus Christ's sake. Amen.

Chapter 2

WHAT MUST I DO TO BE SAVED?

By J. Wilbur Chapman

Sirs, what must I do to be saved? And they said, Believe on the Lord Jesus Christ and thou shalt be saved. – Acts 16:30-31

The apostle Paul lived in a perpetual state of revival. He only had to enter Philippi, the principal city of Macedonia, and sit by the riverbank, and Lydia, the seller of purple, immediately believed and was baptized (Acts 16:13-15). He only had to walk along the streets to the place of prayer, and there was so much power about him that *a certain damsel possessed with the spirit of divination* followed him and cried, saying,

These men are the servants of the most high God; and Paul, being grieved, turned and said to the spirit, I command thee in the name of Jesus Christ to come out of her. And he came out the same hour. And when her masters saw that the hope of their gains was gone, they caught Paul and Silas and drew them into the market-place (Acts 16:16-19). Then they tore off their clothes, beat them with many stripes, and cast them into the inner prison, fastening their feet in the stocks; but this did not in any way affect these servants of God. It was undoubtedly true for them, as one of the modern poets has expressed, "Stone walls did not a prison make, nor iron bars a cage,"[3] for at midnight in the midst of all the darkness, they *sang praises unto God: and the prisoners heard them* (Acts 16:25).

What a strange sound that must have been in that old jail, where ordinarily only curses had been heard! But *suddenly there was a great earthquake, so that the foundations of the prison were shaken: and immediately all the doors were opened, and every one's bands were loosed* (Acts 16:26). In the midst of all this confusion, the jailer sprang into their presence and was ready to kill himself, thinking the prisoners had escaped. Paul then exclaimed, *Do thyself no harm: for we are all here* (Acts 16:28).

Right in this connection there is a clear distinction drawn between men of influence and men of power. Ordinarily, we say that what the church needs today is men of influence, meaning men of position; and so it

---

3   This was written by Richard Lovelace in 1642 in his poem "To Althea, from Prison."

does. But from this illustration, I think we may agree that the greater demand is for men of power.

Paul and Silas did not have enough influence to keep them out of jail, but they had power that was sufficient to pray down the prison walls and throw wide open its doors. Also in this incident, there is given to us a true and noticeable picture of what it means for one to be saved.

If I were an artist, I would like to draw upon a blackboard a large letter "C," and then fill out from that one letter four words. These four words would present to us not only a picture of this Philippian jailer, but also of everyone who really and truly comes to Christ.

CONVICTION

The first word would be "Conviction." We certainly find this in the jailer, for we are told that he *came trembling* (Acts 16:29). It is not possible for anyone to be saved without first of all experiencing real conviction. However, it should be suggested that this may manifest itself in different ways in different people.

> It is not possible for anyone to be saved without first experiencing real conviction.

Sometimes it is evidenced in great need. One would display his ignorance if he were to assert that Nicodemus, for example, was the chief of sinners, for he was a ruler of his people, an honored member of the Sanhedrin, and a most vigilant man in every way; but there was a great sense of a need in his heart that his position had never satisfied, and this compelled him, I imagine, to seek out the Great Teacher.

If, therefore, there is this feeling in your heart today that the world does not satisfy, that the pleasures of sin prove to be a mockery, and if with all this there is a sense of need you have not yet had satisfied, this may be real conviction. Come to Jesus with that need. He alone can help you.

Not infrequently it may assume the form of complete unworthiness, such as the poor publican had when he said, *God be merciful to me, a sinner* (Luke 18:13); but the article there in the Greek was a definite one, and what he really said was this: "God be merciful to me, *the* sinner," as if he were the only one in the world. This is a most hopeful condition.

As a rule, it is the awareness that we have sinned, and are therefore under condemnation. In the unregenerate state, it is the fearfulness that the penalty of the broken law may fall upon us, yet I am quite clear in my own mind that there may be a deeper conviction of one's sins after one's regeneration than before.

Just as one may not be aware that their face is dirty until they look in a mirror, in a similar way, many people can never know what sin is until they see it in the presence of Jesus Christ. But whatever the form of conviction, it must surely be experienced before the light will dawn. Come to Jesus just as you are, for He can satisfy your longings by filling you with Himself, and He is able to blot out all your transgressions and forgive all your sins.

CONTRITION

The second word starting with the letter "C" would be "Contrition." The Philippian jailer had this, for he *fell down before Paul and Silas* (Acts 16:29). It is certainly true that one cannot come to God without first of all having a broken and contrite heart. Why would this not be true? We have sinned against God, and there must be contrition (remorse, shame, and repentance) for it if we are to be forgiven. God may be ever so willing to forgive, but still He does not do so without contrition.

In the state prison of Iowa, there is a young man held as a convict against whom the charge of arson stands, and also the attempt to kill. Very recently, the party whose building was set on fire circulated a petition stating that the young man should be pardoned. The man whose life was attempted followed his example and succeeded in securing the names of the judge by whom he was sentenced, the attorney who prosecuted him, and the entire jury that found him guilty. This petition was carried to the governor. In the face of it, as strong as it was, he said, "No, the man cannot be pardoned, for his crime was not committed against the individual, but against the commonwealth of Iowa, and he must serve his sentence."

> God may be ever so willing to forgive, but still He does not do so without your contrition.

It should be remembered by the sinner that these words are true: *Against thee, thee only, have I sinned* (Psalm 51:4). There must be contrition, or there cannot be salvation; yet what a marvelous thing it is that if someone is ever so great a sinner, the moment this spirit is manifest, God blots out all his transgressions.

It is stated that in St. Petersburg, a father's heart was nearly broken because of the prodigality of his son, who was addicted to the habit of gambling – and with that came the accompanying vices. At last the old father came up with the idea that what the boy needed was better surroundings, so he set out to secure them. What a mistake this is, and how many have made it! That is not what you need.

The other day, a woman was seated in Central Park, New York, with her little child playing near her, when suddenly she was startled by the shrieking of the little one. She had been frightened by the barking of a dog, and she jumped into her mother's arms, who sought to comfort her by saying, "The dog has stopped barking. Why are you afraid?" The child only sobbed out, "But Mama, the bark is still in him." This is true of people in sin. The bark is still in them, and what they need is not new surroundings, but a new nature. This comes only from above and can be received only by faith.

Anyway, this father of whom I speak secured his son's appointment in the army, but in this position he went from bad to worse until he had reached the end of it all. He was completely discouraged. He was figuring up all the money he owed, and when the overwhelming figure was reached, in great desperation he wrote at the bottom of the column these words: "Who is to pay all this?"

The emperor of Russia, as was his habit, went through the barracks to inspect the soldiers. He passed this young man, who had fallen asleep with his head in his arms. The emperor glanced at the figures before him on the table, read the question, and then bent over and wrote one word: "Nicholas." And as the story goes, that one name meant the cancelling of all the indebtedness, and the man was free.

I do not know if this story is true, but I do know that if you list all of your sins from the earliest recollection to the present moment, and beneath the sum of them all, write this question, "Who is to pay all this?" there will be one name written in answer to it:

> Sweetest note in seraph song,
>   Sweetest name on mortal tongue;
> Sweetest carol ever sung,
>   Jesus, blessed Jesus.[4]

CONVERSION

The third word that begins with the letter "C" would be "Conversion," and we find this in the Philippian jailer, for we are told that he *washed their stripes* (Acts 16:33). This was certainly a great change in the man.

At first, he pleasingly fastened their feet in the stocks. I can imagine him then stooping down with a cooling touch to ease their pain. There must be conversion if we are ever to be saved. I am not speaking of the new birth – that is God's part of it – but I am emphasizing the thing man must do if he is ever to see the light.

In one way it is, "Right, about face!" It is following

---

4   This is the refrain from the hymn written by William Hunter (1811-1877) that begins with "The great Physician now is near."

the example of the blind men who put themselves in the way of Jesus, or it is the obedience of the lepers who, as they went, were cleansed. Indeed, to sum it all up, it is for the unsaved person to have the willing mind. We are told that if we are willing and obedient, we *shall eat the good of the land* (Isaiah 1:19). God never saved anyone until first of all he was willing to be saved. So whether one kneels at the altar, bows in prayer in his own home, stands in the crowded audience, or signs the inquirer's card, the end of all these things must be the submission of the will to God; then God does His own work, and we are born again – born from above.

God never saved anyone until first of all he was willing to be saved.

CONFESSION

The fourth and last word to be completed from the letter "C" is "Confession," and this is clearly found in the experience of the jailer, for we are told that he *was baptized* (Acts 16:33). What a mistake it is for a person to believe in his heart, yet fail to confess with his lips! Such a position is never satisfactory and never brings real joy. It is not being obedient, to say the least.

If your physician would write two prescriptions for you in your sickness, but you only took one of the medication he prescribed, he would have the right to find fault with you and tell you that you would never get well until you took the entire prescription. It is the same with the Great Physician in our sin sickness. He has written the prescription that assures us of life, and it is composed of two parts:

First: Believe in your heart that Jesus is the Christ, the Son of God.

Second: Confess with your lips that you have appropriated Him, not as *a* Savior, but as *your* Savior, for if one desires to be fully saved, he must commit himself (Romans 10:9). It is not walking with the army that makes one a soldier; it is not even wearing the uniform of a soldier that makes him such, for this may be bought or stolen, but it is the definite enlistment, and this comes to one who would be a soldier of Jesus Christ when he definitely and clearly confesses Him. This is his enlistment.

What must I do to be saved? This seems to be the unsaved person's first question. Philosophy has never yet answered this question. Unbelief has tried it and has made it a mockery. God's answer is clear and simple. The Bible says, *By grace are ye saved through faith; and that not of yourselves: it is the gift of God. Not of works, lest any man should boast* (Ephesians 2:8-9). It is very easy to receive a gift. The first step in salvation is not to give something, but rather to receive.

Man would naturally say that if you want to be a child of God, try to walk as a child and you will eventually become one. However, God makes it very clear that there can be no real life until there is a step taken first of all by faith; then He reveals Himself. The things of God are spiritually discerned, and God is a revelation rather than an explanation.

To make it very clear, the best answer is the one

given: *Believe on the Lord Jesus Christ, and thou shalt be saved* (Acts 16:31).

THE NAMES OF JESUS CHRIST

There is something very significant in the way the names of Jesus Christ are used. For example, when He is called "Lord," it is to emphasize His kingly office, or His reigning power, and what can the meaning be except when we are told to believe on Him as Lord? We must reach the place where we are willing to let Him reign in our lives. Can you submit to this? He will never make a failure of it.

"Jesus" is His earthly name, and the Bible says, *Thou shalt call his name Jesus: for he shall save his people from their sins* (Matthew 1:21). It must be necessary, then, for us to get a perception of Him as He hangs upon the cross, and certainly we know He was there for just one purpose: that He might die in our place (1 Peter 2:24).

Major Whittle tells the story of a company of robbers arrested in Missouri during the days of the war. They were sentenced to be shot. The punishment was about to be carried out when a young boy touched the commanding officer on the arm and said, "Won't you allow me to take the place of the man standing over there? He has a family and will be greatly missed. No one will miss me; may I take his place?" When the officer had given his consent, the young boy stepped forward, took the man out of line, and stood in his place. When the command was given to fire, the boy fell down dead. His grave is still to be found in the little Missouri town, and on the stone that marks it is cut these words: "Sacred to the memory of Willie Lear. He took my place."

This is true of Jesus Christ. He died so that we might live, but we must accept Him. He is also called "Christ," but this is His resurrection name. As Christ, He stands this moment at the right hand of God and is interceding for us. Can you accept Him there?

It seems to me that this makes the whole Christian life very plain. Jesus is my Lord because He rules me. He is Jesus because He saved me. He is Christ because whenever the mistakes of life overtake me, He stands at God's right hand to make explanation and intercession. Do you receive Him in this way?

THE WORD OF GOD

It is also to be remembered that in the case of the Philippian jailer, light came in all its clearness when *they spake unto him the word of the Lord* (Acts 16:32).

I have very little confidence in that person who is not established upon God's Word for the assurance of his salvation. I have all the hope imaginable for that person who will receive it with meekness. I do not mean that he should be able to explain it immediately, but only that he receives it by faith.

> I have little confidence in that person who is not established upon God's Word for the assurance of his salvation.

God's Word is sometimes spoken of under the figure of the hammer (e.g., Jeremiah 23:29), and as such it can break our stubborn wills. It is sometimes said to be the light (e.g., Psalm 119:105), and as such it will penetrate the darkness. It is frequently called the water (e.g., Ephesians 5:26) for it always cleanses by displacement. I am convinced that if we only persuade people to receive the Word of God, it would bring joy unspeakable and a peace that the world can neither give nor take away.

One could not live in the promise and declaration of John's third chapter, sixteenth verse, without rejoicing in hope. Say it over and over to yourself this way, and thus make it your own verse: *God so loved [me], that He gave His only begotten Son, that [I] believing in Him should not perish, but have everlasting life.*

I do not want you to forget that in this interesting story of the jailer, he was baptized. Baptism is inseparably connected with believing, and it is just as certainly a command of God's as that we believe.

We may differ as to the mode, but too much emphasis cannot be placed upon the command itself. It is true, of course, that one may be saved without it, as, for example, the thief on the cross. For him, it was impossible, but I would be afraid to run the risk when Jesus said, *He that believeth and is baptized shall be saved; but he that believeth not shall be damned* (Mark 16:16).

Baptism is just as certainly a command of God's as that we believe.

Eventually when we stand before Him, we could not but say that we had neglected to do as He commanded if we have not been baptized. It is the experience of Christians everywhere that this sacrament brings upon the believer a marvelous blessing and leads him out into an experience that can never be described in words.

REJOICED

It is not to be forgotten that when all these steps had been taken by the Philippian jailer, he *rejoiced, believing in God with all his house* (Acts 16:34). That word is certainly true that in His presence is fullness of joy, and at His right hand there are *pleasures for evermore* (Psalm 16:11).

And why should it not be so?

One of my friends, a Scotsman, told me that some time ago he was going through his native land and stopped at a little cottage by the wayside to rest. When he entered the room, his first inclination was to be seated in a very comfortable chair that occupied a very prominent place in the room. However, just as he made the attempt, an old Scottish woman ran to the chair, lifted her hand, and exclaimed, "Nay, nay, man, don't sit there," and she pointed to the scarlet cord fastened around the chair that he had not noticed before. She then said, "One day as Her Majesty, the queen, was traveling, a sudden storm came upon her, and she left her carriage and came into this house." With a look of great reverence, the woman exclaimed, "She sat in this chair. After she left, we fastened this scarlet cord around it, and I said, 'We will give it to John, and he can keep it in his family.'" She then said, "Is it not wonderful that Her Majesty, the queen, has used it?"

But I have a greater cause for rejoicing. Jesus Christ,

the King of Kings, has counted it a joy to take up His residence in my heart. He has cast around me the scarlet cord, which makes me as His own. It is a great thing for me to say that He is mine, but it is far greater for me to declare that I am His, and with the Philippian jailer, therefore, I rejoice with exceeding great joy.

Chapter 3

THE OLD TESTAMENT PRODIGAL

By John McNeill

My text is Psalm 119, verses 59 and 60: *I thought on my ways, and turned my feet unto thy testimonies. I made haste, and delayed not to keep thy commandments.* That is what I call the Old Testament story of the prodigal son. All that you have in the New Testament with the circumstances and details is condensed into this brief abstract from the man who wrote the psalms.

I thought on my ways. This is explained in detail in the New Testament, but here it is implied rather than expressed. However, both there and here you have the history of a man who once lived at home, but who wandered away into shame and folly. Then, when he came to himself, he went back again to all blessedness for this world and the next.

This would have done splendidly as a headstone to set over the grave of the returned prodigal of Christ's story when he died, for Christ has told us about the young man so vividly that we have long ago stopped seeing him as a mere lay figure in a story. He has become real to us, and I often suppose that after this young fellow came home, he stayed home and did well and perhaps eventually got the whole estate into his hands. He outlived his father and his elder brother, and at last, filled with honors, he lay down and died.

When you think of him dead and buried, and if they put up headstones there as we do here, we cannot imagine anything more appropriate to inscribe upon the tombstone of the departed prodigal than from our text: "Here lies one who thought on his ways, and turned his feet unto God's testimonies, and made haste, and delayed not to keep His commandments."

This is the record of an experience. May the Lord grant that we may find, as we go through it, that we are occupying ourselves with our own experience; and if it has not been so with ourselves until now, may we begin the experience recorded here at once.

SPIRITUAL DIARIES

To change the illustration, this text is an entry in the spiritual diary of the man who wrote the psalms. It is one of those little autobiographical touches that make the psalms so true and give them their perennial interest.

They so often, like all true poetry, come down to our level, and we say, "I might have said that myself!" Like Columbus and the egg, it is quite easy if you know how.

I thought on my own ways, and turned my feet unto thy testimonies. I made haste, and delayed not to keep thy commandments. I might have said that myself. I hope I can say it myself now that David and the Holy Spirit behind him have started me. Do you keep a diary? Whether you do or not, God does. Has God had good reason to write in that impartial record of your life that He is keeping such an entry as this on a particular day? Possibly. Only God knows, for as a man may be born and not be able to tell either the place or the hour, but the fact of his existence is conclusive that it happened somehow, sometime – so a man may be born again and not know the time nor the place; but does God know?

That is the point. Has the fact happened of your spiritual birth, of your conversion, and of your return to God? Has He had good reason to enter in the record that He keeps some such entry as this, that on such and such a day, you, John Brown, thought on your ways, turned your feet, and made haste and did not delay to return to God in Christ for pardon and eternal life? It is time the record was in, for in the case of the best of us, naturally speaking, there are enough dark and shameful entries to make that record bitter reading in the day when the judgment will be set and the books opened, and the dead judged out of the things that are written in the book (Revelation 20:12). That red-letter entry will redeem the record, and it is time it was there.

I AM NOT A PRODIGAL

But I can imagine somebody saying, "Ah, this does not apply to me. The preacher is evidently going to give a discourse based upon the prodigal son," and you say that you are not a prodigal. My friend, you have wandered away. You are either on the outgoing journey from God, headed into ever deepening darkness, or you are on the ingoing journey back to God and holiness and heaven. Wandering from God is not something any of us still are to do, for the wandering is already done. The great question is: Have we started heading home?

You are either on the outgoing journey from God or you are on the ingoing journey back to God.

We go astray from the womb. We could not go earlier, but we go then. We are born wrong. *All we like sheep have gone astray; we have turned every one to his own way; and the LORD hath laid on him the iniquity of us all* (Isaiah 53:6). Some of us go blundering on through the mud and mire of drunkenness, swearing, immorality, and open sinning; that is our way to the far country. Some of us go along the paved road of self-righteousness, churchgoing, and sermon-hearing; that is our way to the same outer darkness.

On which path are you? Consider the path of your feet. *Thus saith the LORD of hosts: Consider your ways* (Haggai 1:7).

THINKING FOR ONESELF

Now when we come to this tremendously astonishing experience for every soul that ever was born, there are two or three things in it, and I want you to notice them. First of all, notice that in this experience of the psalmist, so succinctly but expressively described here, is a man first of all who thinks for himself: *I thought.* I wish I had a voice like a trumpet so I could ring it in the ears of all the world that the beginning of all blessedness lies in this little root. Just as mighty oaks come out of little acorns, so the mighty and glorious tree of everlasting life grows out of this little seedling of personal thinking.

It is because salvation, in the large meaning of that biblical expression, begins down there that the kingdom of God goes on so slowly. It is because there is no group work, no mass work, no priestly work, no getting into heaven in batches and squadrons and regiments, no tricks and magic, that you are not saved. It is because we must begin, every one of us, down here that so few find everlasting life. Religion is not magic; it is a daylight business. It is open and honest and is done in the daylight of a clear understanding. Bring your best mind with you when you come to hear God's Word.

While the stream of our sermon is flowing, the mill wheel of your thinking is going; but when the stream is shut off, when the sermon stops, how long does the wheel – the mill wheel of your personal independent thought about the things of God and your own eternal destiny – how long does it keep working?

You cannot get anybody to do your thinking for you. It is not, "I thought about the sermon," but, "I thought about my ways." No one can know the inmost thoughts of your heart. Your own soul is the issue at stake, and the thinking that will save it must be done by that soul's powers themselves.

My text is not so easy if you take it properly. I do not doubt that people think that is a kind of cheap, almost flimsy utterance of Scripture. Is it? It is widening and deepening. There is room in it for the head and shoulders, the heart, and the hands and feet of an immortal man, and may God help you to put yourself right in. It needs a saved person to widen out verses 59 and 60 of Psalm 119 to their true and largest proportion.

Yes, the beginning lies in personal thinking: *I thought.* I know quite well that in the affairs of this world, many of us make it our boast, "I think for myself." You are not led by the nose by anybody. You would not trust me to go around the corner with a message for you, and that is making your fortune. You are picking up a fortune from under the feet of careless, happy-go-lucky, easygoing mortals simply because you think for yourself, you do things for yourself, you set your own eyes on the problem, and you tackle it with your own teeth and your own fingers.

However, the tremendous accusation that I have against some wise men and women is that in the things of their eternity, the devil himself might pity them because they are so absolutely destitute of serious personal thinking. Yes, I repeat it: the devil might pity them. They are so near, so close, and they would be right with just a little consideration; yet they are such worlds away, for they never began to think for themselves about their own soul. You must do your own thinking, and turn your own soul, and go back to God on your own feet. We go astray one by one, and we go back each man separately, and each woman separately.

THINKING ABOUT ONESELF

Now the next thing about this wonderful experience is that he not only thought *for* himself, but secondly, he thought *about* himself. He basically said, *I thought on my ways* (Psalm 119:59). Here is a man who thought *for* himself *about* himself. When one begins to set himself to do that, there is no more interesting subject for meditation to me than me.

> You must do your own thinking, and turn your own soul, and go back to God.

I am interested in you, and I am interested in my friend, but I am selfish enough to admit that John is a great subject of interest to McNeill, and we have often had little chats together. I wish we had more time to have more, and my danger is that I am neglecting my own ways for looking after yours. *I thought on my ways.*

Now there is somebody here tonight who is losing the benefit of this sermon because even while I am talking, the devil is defeating you by this trick. While I am talking to you, you are looking across this building, either actually or mentally, at somebody who is here, and the moment you meet outside you will say, "I am glad you were here; that sermon was for you." You will say to them, "I hope you listened to him. Didn't you see me looking at you? You do not get talked to like that every day." So you see, the devil wins again; it is his trump card. Many times you are hoping that the other person is here and are hoping that they are thinking on their ways.

Now be a little "selfish" and consider your own ways first. There is not a soul among us whose ways do not need mending and ending. There is not one of us who could not be somewhat improved. We must directly face God with our backs right up against death and hell.

Or if you are not looking at somebody, you are losing the benefit of this because your mind is turning thoughtfully back to your own house or the house of a friend who is not here, and you will rush away to them, and when you see them, you will say, "Oh, I am so sorry you were not there; it just would have fit you to a T." There is it again.

Now before you rush to your friend, I wish you would put your own ways right. Do you think, my decent friend, that you are right yourself? Are you? Maybe your friend is bad, and he very likely already knows that himself. He wants to know how to be put right, and he wants you to tell him, but you have never told him yet. That is the dry rot of practical religion.

I thought on my ways. Oh, speak to your own heart. You do not need a hundred of the best books to do this kind of thinking. You do not need a library or the benefit of clergy at all, but sit down with your own conscience and your own record. Sit down and put your own soul in a corner. Talk to your heart. Say to yourself, "My soul, I must speak with you. Listen." Say to yourself, "John, answer me – where do you think a man in your situation and knowledge will end up? Soul, you have been tricking me. Soul, you have been avoiding this. You have been ignoring eternal truths, but I will have you listen now." That is how to talk to yourself.

May God help you preach to yourself a sermon that no mortal minister can ever preach. Let memory bring out of past years what memory contains of your own life. Talk to yourself until your face grows white with fear upon your bed. Do not lose your soul because I or some other poor minister cannot work miracles and preach a soul-awakening sermon and say the tremendously personal stirring things that only God and your own heart know. Talk to yourself, and you will be converted before night, unless you are a fool.

THREE CHANNELS OF PERSONAL THINKING

When a person begins to think about his ways, there are three channels into which he may turn the direction of his personal independent thinking. First, *Who am I?* The Bible and my own conscience give the only and the sure answer to the question, What is man? Philosophy and science cannot tell. Between the covers of the Bible, I can learn that I am an immortal soul, a living, thinking, spiritual being surrounded by the material for awhile, but rising above it. God breathed into our nostrils the breath of life, and man became a living being (Genesis 2:7), born never, never, to go out of existence.

Secondly, *Where am I?* You are on the most uncertain footing you can imagine. You are here today and gone tomorrow. *Man dieth, and wasteth away: yea, man giveth up the ghost, and where is he?* (Job 14:10). A little while ago, a wave out of the past eternity casts us up like driftwood on the shores of time; and a little while ahead, a wave from the eternity that is coming will carry us into the future. We cannot be certain of twenty-four hours ahead. Such is the life of man. God grant that we may shape ourselves for the great eternity. An elderly man said long ago, "Turn to God the day before you die."

"But," said his disciples, "we do not know the day of our death."

"Therefore," he replied, "turn to God today."

Thirdly, *Where am I going?* The Bible tells us that we must all appear before the judgment seat of Christ. Think of it! Every individual soul must appear in the blinding blaze of light that streams from the judgment seat of Christ. That is where we are going first, and then the eternal doom! Heaven or hell. We will see Him, and He will say, *Come, ye blessed* (Matthew 25:34), or *Depart from me, ye cursed* (Matthew 25:41). May God grant that we may not fear to meet Jesus.

A PRACTICAL THINKER

Further, I want you to notice another point. This is a man who not only thought *upon* himself and *about* himself, but in the third place, he was *a practical thinker.* He said, *I thought on my ways, and turned my feet.* We look at God's words as if they were nothing, and we take and roll them under our tongue until they get smooth and thin.

> The coin grows smooth in traffic current passed,
> Till Caesar's image is effaced at last.[5]

He was a practical thinker, for he said, *I . . . turned my feet.* This sermon will go the way of so many you have heard unless some (and I will neither call you a saint, nor a sinner, nor a backslider; I will just call you brother man and sister woman) will say, "Soul, will you turn now?"

I thought on my ways, and turned my feet. The young prodigal could have sat and felt sorry for himself with the grunting swine until he had died. He not only deplored himself and called himself a fool and formed good resolutions, but he arose on the same two feet that led him away, trudged back again to his father, and became a humbler youth – and that is the point.

It is a humbling thing to admit that you need to turn.

What is the great difficulty in conversion? I will tell you in a word. It is simply because it is going back. It is a humbling thing to admit that you need to turn and that the evangelical preachers were right and you were a conceited fool. Now that is humbling. Why is it that with some of you dear, decent people who are turned (shall I say forty years of age?) and have a

---

5   These are lines from "The Progress of Error," a poem by William Cowper (1731-1800).

good character, credit, and reputation, especially of a churchgoing and chapel-going kind – why is it that the likelihood of your genuine conversion to God (you are not converted yet, and you know it) becomes less and less every year? I will tell you why: it is because it would be so humbling.

You have dared to speak about real, living religion. You have dared to say something like this: "Ah, I don't believe in these people who go about saying that they are saved." I know people can do that foolishly, but it is not all folly, and the thing's right at bottom. If you get converted, you will see. It will come out. It cannot be hidden. It will tell in a thousand ways before next Sunday. You will tell it yourself, and then we will all understand.

That is what the devil is whispering in someone's ear while I am at the other. You are just about ready to go my way, but the devil whispers, "Everyone will hear about this, and we will all understand that when you dared to criticize converted people, you are as much worth listening to as a blind man who would talk about painting, or as a deaf man who would talk about music." You are rambling about things that are as high as heaven above you, and as deep as hell beneath your shallow soul. But as bitter as the experience may be, God will help you to go through it. It is a bitter pill to be converted, but just like the young fellow going home, notice that he was wrestling with himself beside the grunting swine. Many poor prodigals do not come back, and it is pride that keeps them in the gutter. "I will not give in. I will not go home to my father. I may become impoverished and battered and ragged, but I will never go back!" And he dies in the swine tub.

See that you are not like him. If you get bitter pills from your doctor, he will very likely give you advice with them: "Never chew your pills. Don't take time to think about them." *I thought on my ways, and turned.*

I wish I could make it plainer, but you see that I cannot. The feet, those outgoing energies, those powers, or symbols of the powers, by which I carry myself beyond myself to actions and customs and places – those powers that the world and the devil and the flesh use are precisely the powers by which I go back to God. The poor prodigal went back on the same feet – bare, bleeding, torn, tanned, and limping, but he went back. I see him that night after the feast when he sat down before he went to bed and looked at himself and saw what a wreck he was, but he said, "Bless God, I am home. Bless God, I am back, saved. Hallelujah! Home! Home! All that dark and scorching path is behind me, and heaven and peace and a welcome are all around me."

My friend, turn your feet; that is the thing. May God hurry you to do it. As old Richard Baxter said, "It is turn or burn."[6]

A TURNING POINT

There are two things: there is a turning point, and there is a turning time. What is the turning point in your outward-bound life? I will tell you. Every summer in

---

6   *The Reformed Pastor* and *A Call to the Unconverted to Turn and Live*, two books by Richard Baxter (1615-1691), are available from Aneko Press.

London, we took our Sunday school children out to the country, and when we had the little creatures there out on the grand field, they ran races with us and themselves. We had the little ones in a line, and then I went away down the field. Then I yelled back to the intending runners and said, "I am the turning post. You run out to me, run around me, and then run back in again as fast as you can to the finish line." I didn't see any little runners that afternoon going about like geese, asking, "Where is the turning point? Where are we to turn?" They could not mistake me.

What is the turning point in every hell-bound life? It is a man, and Jesus Christ is such a man, standing between us and the hell we want to avoid and deserve to be in, saying to us, "Don't go down there. It is a terrible road. *Turn ye, turn ye from your evil ways, for why will ye die?" As I live, saith the Lord God, I have no pleasure in the death of the wicked; but that the wicked turn from his way and live* (Ezekiel 33:11). That is an oath from God.

"Live?" you say. "If I turn to God, He will kill me. If I turn to God and become religious, it is death." No, it is not. He says, "Turn unto Me and live" – live! That is the turning point – Jesus Christ – there before your mind, as visible to your understanding as this book is to your face, and far more powerful. Don't you almost feel the pat of His hand on your shoulder as He tries to stop you and say, "Turn. Stop at Me and go back with Me to My Father and your Father, My heaven and your home"? Decide for Christ. Stop at Christ.

In evil long I took delight
    Unawed by guilt or fear,
Till a new object met my sight
    And stopped my wild career;

I saw One hanging on the cross
    In agonies and blood,
Who fixed His dying eyes on me,
    As near that cross I stood.[7]

Ah, that is the sight to stop you! Until you have seen Christ on the cross, you will cheerfully go to the devil, and you will take your own way to him, but that is the essence of it. You may say, "It is not," but that is where it ends. However, when your eyes open to see Jesus, you cannot go past Him. May it be done now. Stop and turn at the living Christ, who once died, and now lives to convert you and save you.

A TURNING TIME

He said, *I made haste, and delayed not.* There is a turning point, and it is Christ. There is a turning time, and it is now – quicker than now if I could express it. *I made haste, and delayed not.* He said it twice. He is so anxious to bring out the necessity of a speedy decision, firmness, and a stand taken, that he says, *I made*

---

7   This are stanzas from a hymn by John Newton (1725-1807), author of "Amazing Grace."

haste, and delayed not. That includes sharpness and promptitude. Young fellow, look here! Suppose this was an address upon success in life. What divisions would I have taken other than the same divisions that I have taken here? If you want to be successful in life, think for yourself about your own business. Be practical and prompt. When you have surveyed the field, make the risk. In all legitimate dealing, there is a point where the risk has to be run. So with eternity, be prompt – now. *I made haste, and delayed not.*

INSTANTANEOUS CONVERSION

Somebody may object and say, "But preacher, that is too sudden. That is instantaneous conversion, and you know, preacher, I have often spoken against instantaneous conversion." But I know you have often spoken about things you know nothing about; that is your trouble. Instantaneous conversion! My friend, your objection is futile. When you fell into the lake last summer, I think you wanted instantaneous salvation from drowning, didn't you? And I rather think you were in earnest about it.

Another of your statements is that you object to earnestness in religion, but that day, you cried out earnestly to be saved from drowning. It wasn't a very artistic performance, but there was a fine whole-souled earnestness about it. If you had the same concern about your soul, you would be heard in heaven, and God's right arm would save you. Instantaneous conversion! That is what we want from earthly dangers. You do not want a committee to go and stand by the edge of the lake and discuss the situation, and then appoint a subcommittee with a chairman to make an interim report. You do not want anybody to go and say, "You fool! How did you get in there?"

No! Instead, you want somebody to go and pull you out first, and afterward discuss the folly or otherwise of getting in. That is what I am doing now. Suppose I said, "Yes, you are right. You are such a cantankerous, twisted old sinner. You are so utterly crooked that God cannot put you straight in less than twenty-four hours of stretching on the tenterhooks[8] of remorse and agony for your sin."

Oh, how quickly you would reply to me and say, "Preacher, that is no salvation at all. Before twenty-four hours, I may be dead and doomed. Can't I be saved now?" And it is infinitely low, to give it no other name, to object to the only cure.

One spring, I was in Plymouth in the south of England. Standing there where you can look away out to Eddystone Lighthouse, I saw a thousand soldiers gathered on the parade ground. By one voice of command, these thousand men – every man of whom wore his head above his shoulder, every man had his own arms and limbs and intellectual and moral powers and faculties – a thousand men were going in one direction, when at the voice of one man, a thousand men stopped. You say, "Many men, many minds." Ah, but not in the army. You will be shot in the army for your independent criticism. "Many men, one mind," if you are wise. A thousand men stopped. At another voice of command, a thousand men

---

8   Tenterhooks were hooked nails used in a tenter, a wooden frame used to make and stretch wool cloth.

turned completely around in the opposite direction, and at another pealing cry, quicker than I am taking time to tell it, a thousand individuals, intelligent men, were walking in a direction completely opposite to that which they had taken sixty seconds before.

Will man have such power over man, and will not God have power to stop – to turn from darkness into light – the creatures who lie in His hand like clay on the potter's wheel? **We are only clay, but God pity us, we are rebellious clay.** Oh, while God is appealing, yield to the appeal of omnipotence. If you let God stop you, you will be stopped and turned.

DECIDE NOW

Don't you hear the footsteps of Death coming quickly behind you? *In such an hour as ye think not* (Matthew 24:44), Death will spring upon you, and how will it be with you then? What if you have the experience of John Paton, the missionary to the New Hebrides? Suppose you had been his wife, and were there absorbed in your work and in your husband's work, full of life and full of hope, when suddenly, from behind, a savage buried a tomahawk in your back and with another stroke nearly severed your head from the body? Death, whether it comes soon or late, tomahawks us suddenly like that.

Make haste. Let there be no delay in turning to God. Decide for Christ now! *Now is the accepted time; behold, now is the day of salvation* (2 Corinthians 6:2). Turn, turn, for why will you die?

Chapter 4

THE GREAT ARBITRATION CASE

By Charles H. Spurgeon

*Neither is there any daysman betwixt us,
that might lay his hand upon us both.*
– Job 9:33

What Job desired to have, the Lord has provided for us in the person of His own dear Son, Jesus Christ. We cannot say with Job that there is no daysman, or arbiter, who can lay his hand upon both, because there is now *one mediator between God and men, the man Christ Jesus* (1 Timothy 2:5). Let us rejoice in Him, if indeed we have an interest in Him; and if we have not yet received Him, may almighty grace bring us even now to accept Him as our Advocate and Friend.

There is an old quarrel between the thrice Holy God and His sinful subjects, the sons of Adam. Man has sinned. He has broken every part of God's law and has recklessly cast off from him the allegiance that is due to his Maker and his King. There is a suit against man, which was formally instituted at Sinai and must be pleaded in court before the Judge of the living and the dead. God is the great plaintiff against His sinful creatures, who are the defendants. If that suit is carried into court, it will go against the sinner. There is no hope whatsoever that at the last tremendous day any sinner will be able to stand in judgment if he leaves the matter of his debts and obligations toward his God unsettled until that dreadful hour.

Sinner, it would be good for you to *agree with thine adversary quickly, whiles thou art in the way* (Matthew 5:25), for once you are delivered up to the great Judge of all the earth, there is not the slightest hope that your suit can be decided in any way other than to your eternal ruin. *Weeping and . . . wailing and gnashing of teeth* (Matthew 13:42; Luke 13:28) will be the doom decided for you forever if your case as before the living God will ever come to be tried at the fiery throne of absolute justice.

However, the infinite grace of God proposes an arbitration, and I believe you are not anxious to have your suit carried into court, but are willing for the appointed Arbiter to stand between you and God and lay His hand upon both and propose and carry out a plan of reconciliation. There is hope for you, you bankrupt sinner, that you may yet be at peace with God. There is a way by which your debts may yet be paid. That way is a blessed arbitration in which Jesus Christ will stand as the Arbiter.

Let me begin by describing the essentials of an arbitrator, or daysman; then let me take you into the arbitrator's court and show you His proceeding; and then for a little time, let us dwell upon the happy success of our great Daysman.

THE ESSENTIAL QUALITIES OF AN ARBITRATOR OR DAYSMAN

The first essential quality is that both parties should be agreed to accept him. Let me come to you, you sinner, against whom God has laid His suit, and put the matter to you. God has accepted Christ Jesus to be His arbiter in His dispute. He appointed Him to the office, and He chose Him for it before He laid the foundations of the world. He is God's fellow, equal with the Most High, and can put His hand upon the Eternal Father without fear because He is dearly beloved of that Father's heart. As the Nicene Creed states, He is "very God of very God," and is in no respect inferior to God over all, *blessed forever* (Romans 9:5).

> Jesus can put His hand upon the Eternal Father without fear because He is dearly beloved of that Father's heart.

But He is also a man like yourself, sinner. He once suffered, hungered, thirsted, and knew the meaning of poverty and pain. He went even farther, for He was tempted as you have been, and farther still, He suffered the pains of death, as you poor mortal man will one day have to do. Now, what do you think? God has accepted Him. Can you agree with God in this matter, and agree to take Christ to be your arbiter too? Does foolish enmity possess you, or does grace reign and lead you to accept Emmanuel, God with us (Matthew 1:23), as arbiter in this great dispute?

Let me say to you that you will never find anyone else of such a kindred spirit to you, so tender, so sympathetic, and with such bowels of compassion toward you. Love streams from His eyes in life, and poured from His wounds in death. He is *the express image* of Jehovah's person (Hebrews 1:3), and you know that Jehovah's name is "Love." *God is love* (1 John 4:8), and Christ is love. Sinner, has divine grace brought you to your senses? Will you accept Christ now? Are you willing for Him to take this case into His hands and arbitrate between you and God? For if God accepts Him, and you accept Him, too, He has one of the first qualifications for being a daysman.

But in the next place, both parties must be fully agreed to leave the case entirely in the arbitrator's hands. If the arbitrator does not possess the power of settling the case, then pleading before him is only making an opportunity for disputing without any chance of coming to a peaceful settlement. Now God has committed *all power* into the hands of His Son (Matthew 28:18). Jesus Christ is the ambassador of God and has been invested with full ambassadorial powers. He comes commissioned by His Father, and He can say that His Father's heart is with

Him in all that He does toward sinners. If the case is settled by Him, the Father is in agreement.

Now, sinner, does grace move your heart to do the same? Will you agree to put your case into the hands of Jesus Christ, the Son of God and the Son of Man? Will you abide by His decision? Will you have it settled according to His judgment, and will the verdict that He gives stand absolute and firm with you? If so, then Christ has another essential quality of an arbitrator; but if not, remember that although He may make peace for others, He will never make peace for you. For know that until the grace of God has made you willing to trust the case in Jesus's hands, there can be no peace for you, and you are willfully remaining God's enemy by refusing to accept His dear Son.

Further, let us say that to make a good arbitrator, it is essential that he is an appropriate person. If the case were between a king and a beggar, it would not seem exactly right that another king or another beggar should be the arbitrator; but if there could be found a person who combined the two, who was both prince and beggar, then such a man could be selected by both.

Our Lord Jesus Christ precisely meets the case. There is a very great disparity between the plaintiff and the defendant, for how great the gulf is that exists between the eternal God and the poor fallen man! How is this to be bridged? This can be bridged by none except by one who is God and who at the same time can become man. The only being who can do this is Jesus Christ. He can put His hand on you, stooping down to all your infirmity and your sorrow, and He can put His other hand upon the Eternal Majesty and claim to be co-equal with God and co-eternal with the Father.

Do you not see, then, His appropriateness? Surely it would be the path of wisdom, sinner, to accept Him at once as the arbitrator in the case. See how well He understands it! I would not be a suitable arbitrator in legal cases because, although I would be anxious to do justice, I would know nothing of the law of the case. But Christ knows your case and the law concerning it because He has lived among men and has passed through and suffered the penalties of justice. There certainly cannot be a better skilled or more judicious arbiter than our blessed Redeemer.

There is one more essential quality of an arbiter, and that is that he should be a person desirous to bring the case to a happy settlement. If you appoint a quarrelsome arbitrator, he may delight to see both sides argue, but if you elect one who is concerned for the good of both and desires to make both friends, then he is just the man, although, to be sure, he would be a man of a thousand, very precious when found, but very hard to find. Oh, that all lawsuits could be decided by such men!

> Jesus knows no joy greater than that of receiving prodigals to His arms.

In the great case that is pending between God and the sinner, the Lord Jesus Christ has a sincere concern both for His Father's glory and for the sinner's welfare, and that there should be peace between the two contending parties. It is the life and aim of Jesus Christ to make peace. He does not delight in the death of sinners, and He knows no joy greater than that of receiving prodigals to His arms and of bringing lost sheep back again to the fold.

You cannot tell how high the Savior's chest swells with an intense desire to make to Himself a great name as a peacemaker. Never has any warrior had such ambition to make war and to win victories therein as Christ has to end war and to win thereby the bloodless triumphs of peace. From the heights of heaven, He came leaping like a young roe down to the plains of earth. From earth, He leaped into the depths of the grave, then up again at a bound He sprang to earth, and up again to heaven. He still does not rest, but presses on in His mighty work to gather in sinners and to reconcile them unto God, making Himself a propitiation for their sins.

You see, then, sinner, how the case is. God has clearly chosen the most appropriate arbitrator. That arbitrator is willing to undertake the case, and you may well place all confidence in Him. But if you will live and die without accepting Him as your arbitrator, then when the case goes against you, you will have no one to blame but yourself. When the everlasting damages will be assessed against you in your soul and body forever, you will have only your own foolishness to curse for having been the cause of your ruin.

May I ask you to speak plainly? Has the Holy Spirit so turned the natural tendency and current of your will so that you have chosen Him because He has first chosen you? Do you feel that Christ this day is standing before God for you? He is God's anointed; is He your elected? God's choice places Him upon you; does your choice agree with that? Remember, where there is no will toward Christ, Christ as yet exercises no saving power. Christ saves no sinner who lives and dies unwilling. He makes unwilling sinners willing before He speaks a word of comfort to them. It is the mark of our election as His people that we are made willing in the day of God's power (Psalm 110:3). Place your hope where God has placed your help – namely, on Christ, who is *mighty to save* (Isaiah 63:1). You cannot have an arbitrator unless both sides are agreed. Do you say, "Yes, yes, with all my soul I choose Him"? Then let us proceed.

Now I want to take you into the court where the trial is going on and show you the legal proceedings before the great Daysman.

The man Christ Jesus (1 Timothy 2:5), *who is over all, God blessed for ever* (Romans 9:5), opens His court by laying down the principles upon which He intends to deliver judgment, and I will now try to explain and expound those principles. They are twofold: first, there is strict justice; and secondly, there is fervent love.

STRICT JUSTICE

The Arbitrator has determined that the case should proceed as it may and that full justice will be done, justice to the very extreme, whether it is for or against the defendant. He intends to take the law in its sternest and severest aspect and to judge according to its strictest letter. He will not be guilty of partiality on either side. If the law says that the sinner shall die, the Arbitrator declares that He will judge that the sinner shall die; and if, on the other hand, the defendant can plead and prove that he is innocent, He intends to rule for him the award of innocence – namely, eternal life. If the sinner can prove that he has fairly won it, he will have his due. Either way, whether it is in favor of the plaintiff or the defendant, the condition of judgment is to be strict justice.

LOVE

But the Arbitrator also says that He will judge according to the second rule – that of fervent love. He loves His Father, and therefore He will decide on nothing that may tarnish His honor or disgrace His crown. He so loves God, the Eternal One, that He will rather allow heaven and earth to pass away than to have one blot upon the character of the Most High. On the other

> **Jesus will be willing to do anything rather than inflict penalty upon man unless justice absolutely requires it.**

hand, He so much loves the poor defendant, man, that He will be willing to do anything rather than inflict penalty upon him unless justice absolutely requires it. He loves man with so much love that nothing will delight Him more than to decide in his favor, and He will be only too glad if He can be the means of happily establishing peace between the two.

How these principles are to meet will be seen eventually. For now, He lays them down very positively. *He that ruleth among men must be just* (2 Samuel 23:3). The Arbitrator must be just, or else He is not fit to hold the scales in any suit. On the other hand, He must be tender, for His name (as God) is love, and His nature (as man) is gentleness and mercy. Both parties should distinctly consent to these principles. How can they do otherwise? Do they not commend themselves to all of you? Let justice and love unite if they can.

THE PLAINTIFF'S CASE

Having thus laid down the principles of judgment, the Arbitrator next calls upon the Plaintiff to state His case. Let us listen while the Great Creator speaks. May God give me grace now reverently to state it in His name, as one poor sinner stating God's case against us all.

> *Hear, O heavens, and give ear, O earth; for the LORD hath spoken, I have nourished and brought up children, and they have rebelled against me. The ox knoweth his owner, and the ass his master's crib: but Israel doth not know. My people doth not consider. Ah sinful nation, a people laden with iniquity, a seed of evildoers, children that are corrupters: they have forsaken the LORD, they have provoked the Holy One of Israel unto anger, they are gone away backward.* (Isaiah 1:2-4)

The Eternal God charges us, and (let me confess at once) most justly and most truly charges us, with having broken all His Commandments – some of them in act, some of them in word, and all of them in heart and thought and imagination. He charges upon us that against light and knowledge, we have chosen the evil and have forsaken the good; that knowing what we were doing, we have turned aside from His most righteous law and have gone astray like lost sheep (Isaiah 53:6), following the imaginations and devices of our own hearts (Jeremiah 18:12).

The great Plaintiff claims that since we are His creatures, we should have obeyed Him, that as we owe our very lives to His daily care, we should have rendered Him service instead of disobedience, and should have been His loyal subjects instead of turning traitors to His throne. All this, calmly and dispassionately, according to the great Book of the Lord, is laid to our charge before the Daysman. No exaggeration of sin is brought against us. It is simply declared of us that *the whole head is sick, and the whole heart faint* (Isaiah 1:5); that *there is none that doeth good, no, not one*; that we have *all gone out of the way* and *are together become unprofitable* (Romans 3:12).

This is God's case. He says, "I made this man; curiously was he *wrought in the lowest parts of the earth* [Psalm 139:15]; and all his parts bear traces of My unique handiwork. I made him for My honor, and he has not honored Me. I created him for My service, and he has not served Me. Twenty, thirty, forty, fifty years I have kept the breath in his nostrils. The bread he has eaten has been the daily portion of My generosity. His garments are the clothing of My kindness. All this happened while he has neither thought of Me, his Creator and Preserver, nor done anything in My service. He has served his family, his wife, and his children, but he has despised his Maker. He has served his country, his neighbors, and the city in which he dwells, but I who made him, I have had nothing from him. He has been an unprofitable servant unto Me."

I think I may put the Plaintiff's case into your hands. Which of you would keep a horse if that horse would not obey you in anything? What excuse is it that although I might not use him, he would carry another? No, the case is worse than this. Not only has man done nothing, but worse than nothing. Which of you would keep a dog that, instead of following you, would bark at you, run at you, and tear you in his rage? Some of us have done this to God. We have perhaps cursed Him to His face. We have broken His sabbaths, laughed at His gospel, and persecuted His saints. You would have said of such a dog, "Let it die. Why should I keep a dog in my house that treats me like that?"

God has put up with your ill manners, and He is still patient with you.

Yet *hear, O heavens; and give ear, O earth* (Isaiah 1:2). God has put up with your ill manners, and He is still patient with you. He puts the lifted thunder back into the arsenal of His dreaded artillery. I wish I could state the case as I should. My lips are but clay, and these words should be like fire in the sinner's soul. When I meditated upon this subject alone, I felt much sympathy with God that He should have been treated so poorly; and whereas some people speak of the flames of hell as too great a punishment for sin, it seems ten thousand marvels that we would not have been thrust down there long ago.

THE DEFENDANT'S CASE

The Plaintiff's case having thus been stated, the defendant is called upon by the Daysman for his, and I think I hear him as he begins. First of all, the trembling sinner pleads, "I confess to the indictment, but I say I could not help it. It is true that I have sinned, but my nature was such that I could not well do otherwise. I must lay all the blame of it to my own heart. My heart was deceitful and my nature was evil."

The Daysman at once rules that this is no excuse whatsoever, but an aggravation; for inasmuch as it is conceded that the man's heart itself is enmity against God, this is an admission of yet greater malice and darker rebellion. It was only alleged against the offender in the first place that he had outwardly offended, but he acknowledges that he does it inwardly, and confesses that his very heart is traitorous against God and is fully set upon working the King's damage and dishonor. It is determined, therefore, by the Daysman, that this excuse will not stand, and He gives a case in point. He says that a thief is brought up for stealing, and he pleads that his heart was thievish, that he felt a constant inclination to steal, and that therefore he could not help running off with any goods within his reach. The judge very properly answers, "Then I will give you twice as much penalty as any other man who only fell into the fault by surprise, for according to your own confession, you are a thief through and through. What you have said is not an excuse, but an aggravation!"

Then the defendant pleads in the next place that although he acknowledges the facts alleged against him, yet he is no worse than other offenders, and he says that there are many in the world who have sinned more grievously than he has done. He says he has been envious, angry, worldly, and covetous, and has forgotten God, but that he was never an adulterer, a thief, a drunkard, or a blasphemer, and he pleads that his lesser crimes may well be overlooked.

But the great Daysman at once turns to the Statute Book, and He says that as He is about to give His decision by law, that plea is not at all defensible, for the Law Book states, *Cursed is every one that continueth not in all things that are written in the book of the law to do them* (Galatians 3:10). The offense of one sinner does not excuse the offense of another; and the Arbitrator declares that He cannot mix up other cases with the case now in hand. The present offender has, by his own confession, broken the law, and that as the Law Book stands, that is the only question to be decided, for *the soul that sinneth, it shall die* (Ezekiel 18:20). If the defendant has no better plea to offer, judgment must go against him.

The sinner argues further that although he has offended, and has offended very greatly and very seriously, yet he has done a great many good things. It is true that he did not love God, but he always went to church. It is true that he did not pray, but still he sang in the choir. It is quite correct that he did not love his neighbor as himself, but he always liked to give to the poor. But the Daysman, looking the sinner directly in the face, tells him that this plea also is bad, for the alleged commission of some acts of loyalty will not compensate for specific acts of treason. He said, "You should have done those things, and not left the other things undone" (Matthew 23:23). He then tells the sinner, with all kindness and gentleness, that straining at a gnat does not excuse him for having swallowed a camel, and that having tithed mint, and anise, and cumin (Matthew 23:23-24) is no justification for having devoured a widow's house (Mark 12:40). To have forgotten God is in itself great wickedness. To have lived without serving Him is a crime of omission so great that whatever the sinner may have done to the contrary stands for nothing at all since he has even then in that case done only what he should have done.

> **To have lived without serving God is a crime of omission.**

You see at once the justice of this decision. If any of you were to say to your grocer or tailor, when they send in their bills, "Well, now, you should not ask for payment of that account because I did pay you another bill. You should not ask me to pay for that suit of clothes because I did pay you for another suit." I think the answer would be, "But in paying for what you had before, you only did what you should have done; but I still have a demand upon you for this."

So all the good deeds you have ever done are only debts discharged that were most fully due (supposing them to be good deeds, which is very questionable), and they leave the great debt still untouched.

The defendant has no end of pleas, for the sinner has a thousand excuses. Realizing that nothing else will do, he begins to appeal to the mercy of the plaintiff, and he says that he will do better in the future. He confesses that he is in debt, but he says that he will run up no more bills at that shop. He acknowledges that he has offended, but he vows not to do so again. He is quite sure that the future will be as free from fault as angels are from sin.

Although it is true that he just said that his heart was bad, still he feels inclined to think that it is not so very bad after all. He is conceited enough to think that he can keep himself from committing sin in the future, thereby, you see, admitting the worthlessness of his former plea on which he relied so much. "Now," he says, "if I abstain from drinking alcohol for the rest of my life, then surely I may be excused for having been a drunkard. Suppose now that I am always honest and steady and never again say one unkind word; will not that exonerate me from all my wrongdoings and for having blasphemed God?"

But the Daysman rules, still with kindness and gentleness, that the greatest imaginable virtue in the future will be no recompense for the sin of the past, for he finds in the law no promise whatsoever made to that effect. Instead, the statute runs in these words: "He will by no means spare the guilty" (Exodus 34:7), and *Cursed is everyone that continueth not in all things which are written in the book of the law to do them* (Galatians 3:10).

PLEADS GUILTY

What is the poor defendant to do now? He is fairly beaten this time. He falls down on his knees, and with many tears and lamentations cries, "I see how the case stands. I have nothing to plead, but I appeal to the mercy of the Plaintiff. I confess that I have broken His commandments. I acknowledge that I deserve His wrath, but I have heard that He is merciful, and I plead for free and full forgiveness."

Now comes another scene. The Plaintiff sees the sinner on his knees, and with His eyes full of tears, makes this reply: "I am willing at all times to deal kindly and according to loving-kindness with all my creatures, but will the Arbitrator for a moment suggest that I should damage and ruin My own perfections of truth and holiness; that I should contradict My own word; that I should imperil My own throne; that I should make the purity of immaculate justice to be suspected, and should bring down the glory of my unblemished holiness because this creature has offended Me and now craves for mercy? I cannot and I will not spare the guilty. He has offended, and he must die! *As I live, . . . I have no pleasure in the death of the wicked*, but would rather that he would turn from his wickedness and live [Ezekiel 33:11]. Still, this 'would rather' must not be supreme. I am gracious and would spare the sinner, but I am just and must not unsay my own words. I swore with an oath, *The soul that sinneth, it shall die* (Ezekiel 18:20). I have laid it down as a matter of firm decree, *Cursed is every one that continueth not in all things which are written in the book of the law to do them* (Galatians 3:10). This sinner is righteously cursed, and he must inevitably die; yet I love him – yet how can I put you among the children? Would it not be a worse calamity if I would be unjust than that the earth would lose its inhabitants? It would be better for all people to perish than that the universe would lose the justice of God as its stay and shield."

THE VERDICT

The Arbitrator bows and says, "Even so; justice demands that the offender should die, and I would not want you to be unjust."

What more does the Arbitrator say? He sits still, and the case is in suspense. There stands the just and holy God, willing to forgive if it can be done without injury to the immutable principles of right. There sits the Arbitrator, looking with eyes of love upon the poor, weeping, trembling sinner, anxious to devise a plan to save him, but knowing that that plan must not infringe upon divine justice; for it would be a worse cruelty to injure divine perfections than it would be to destroy the whole human race.

> It would be better for all people to perish than that the universe would lose the justice of God as its stay and shield.

The Arbitrator, therefore, after pausing awhile, puts it like this: "I am anxious that these two should be brought together. I love them both. I cannot, on the one hand, recommend that My Father should stain His honor. I cannot, on the other hand, endure that this sinner should be cast eternally into hell. I will decide the case, and here is the decision:

I will pay my Father's justice all that it demands. I pledge Myself that in the fullness of time, I will suffer in My own proper person all that the weeping, trembling sinner should have suffered. My Father, will you agree to this?

The eternal God accepts the remarkable sacrifice! What do you say, sinner? What do you say? I do not think you can have two opinions. If you are sane (and may God make you sane), you will melt with wonder. You will say, "I could not have imagined this! I never called in a Daysman with an expectation of this! I have sinned, and He declares that He will suffer. I am guilty, and He says that He will be punished for me!"

CHRIST DIED TO SAVE THE DEFENDANT

Yes, sinner, and He did more than say it, for *when the fullness of the time came, God sent forth His Son* (Galatians 4:4). At the appointed time, the officers of justice served Him with the summons, and He was taken from His knees in the garden of Gethsemane, away to the court, and there He was tried and condemned. You know how His back was scourged until the white bones stood like islands of ivory in the midst of a crimson sea of gore. You know how His head was crowned with thorns, and how His cheeks were given to those who plucked off the hair! Can you not see Him hounded through the streets of Jerusalem, with the spittle of the brutal soldiers still upon His unwashed face, and His wounds all open and bleeding? Can you not see Him as they throw Him down and fasten Him to the accursed tree – and then lift the cross and dash it down into its socket in the earth, dislocating every bone and tearing every nerve and sinew, filling His soul as full of agony as this earth is full of sin, or as the depths of the ocean are filled with its floods?

You do not know, however, what He suffered within. Hell celebrated within His heart. Every arrow of the infernal pit was discharged at Him, and heaven itself forsook Him. The thunderbolts of vengeance fell upon Him, and His Father hid His face from Him because He who knew no sin was made sin for us *that we might be made the righteousness of God in him* (2 Corinthians 5:21), and He cried in His agony, *My God, my God, why hast thou forsaken me?* (Matthew 27:46). And so He suffered on, and on, and on, until *It is finished!* from His dying lips closed the scene (John 19:30).

Here, then, is the arbitration. Christ Himself suffers, and now I must ask the question, "Have you accepted Christ?" Dear friend, if you have, I know that God the Holy Spirit has made you accept Him. But if you have not, what shall I call you? I will not admonish you, but my heart would weep over you. How can you be so irrational as to reject a compromise so blessed, an arbitration so divine! Oh, kiss the feet of the Daysman. Love Him all your life because He has decided the case so blessedly.

I would to God that you would now look to the Savior, that you would come with weeping and tears to Him and say with Charles Wesley,

> Jesus, lover of my soul,
>> Let me to Thy bosom fly.

Tell the Savior, "Take my case, and arbitrate for me. I accept Your atonement. I trust in Your precious blood. Only receive me, and I will rejoice in You forever with *joy unspeakable and full of glory*" (1 Peter 1:8).

May the Lord bless you forevermore. Amen.

Chapter 5

AS THEY WENT

By B. Fay Mills

It came to pass, as he went to Jerusalem, that he passed through the midst of Samaria and Galilee. And as he entered into a certain village, there met him ten men that were lepers, which stood afar off: and they lifted up their voices, and said, Jesus, Master, have mercy on us. And when he saw them, he said unto them, Go show yourselves unto the priests.
– Luke 17:11-14

The priests were the health officers, and these lepers had no right to go to the priests until they knew they were well, and they knew they were not well. But *it came to pass, that, as they went, they were cleansed* (Luke 17:14).

Jesus taught His disciples in three ways: sometimes by direct instruction, sometimes by relating a parable, and sometimes by making use of an illustration, frequently taken from some present object or event. In connection with the practical teaching of the healing of the lepers, He made use of all three of these methods.

The disciples had said to Jesus, *Increase our faith.* In response, He had said to them, *If ye had faith as a grain of mustard seed, ye might say to this sycamore tree, Be thou plucked up by the root, and be thou planted in the sea; and it should obey you* (Luke 17:5-6). Then He told them the parable about the man having a servant, plowing or feeding cattle, and said:

> *Which of you, having a servant plowing or feeding cattle, will say unto him by and by, when he is come from the field, Go and sit down to meat? And would not rather say unto him, Make ready wherewith I may sup, and gird thyself, and serve me, till I have eaten and drunken; and afterward thou shalt eat and drink? Doth he thank that servant because he did the things that were commanded him? I trow not. So likewise ye, when ye shall have done all those things which are commanded you, say, We are unprofitable servants: we have done that which was our duty to do.* (Luke 17:7-10)

This was the answer that He gave to them when they said: *Increase our faith.* It meant practically, "Do the next thing that you should do, in a humble spirit." Then there came this practical and better illustration of the doctrine in the cleansing of the ten lepers.

I want to make the method of God so plain and simple that no one will be able to rise up at the judgment day and say that he was in this meeting and did not learn how he could inherit eternal life. No, I do not have to make it simple. I want to make it as God has made it. I want to tell it as God has told it. I want to strip it of all that men have put around it that has disguised its form – the marvelous simplicity of the way by which people may lay hold of eternal life.

THREE THINGS DUE TO GOD

I believe that God has a right to expect three things of both heathens and Christians. No matter whether a person is born in a gutter or in a palace, in the depths of Africa or in the most Christian city on earth, God has a right to expect of him first, an honest effort to forsake sin; second, a sincere desire to know the truth in order to do it; and third, an open confession of his commitment to righteousness. God has a right to expect

> God has a right to expect an honest effort to forsake sin.

these three things from every person who ever had a mind and a conscience, and doing these three things will lead anybody upon earth into the eternal light and life of God. It is just as simple as that. As they go, they will be cleansed. Let me analyze this a little.

First, an honest effort to forsake sin does not mean

to forsake sin that you do not know, but it means to forsake everything that you do know that is sinful. It also means that you will adopt the principle that as you get more light that shows you more uncleanness in the heart, you will also give that up.

Second, you will have an honest desire to know the truth in order to do it. I believe that one of the most cursed ambitions that ever stirred a human mind is a selfish desire for knowledge. To desire simply to know may be a devilish thing, but to know in order to do is a godly thing – a passion for knowledge for the sake of character, to live up to all the light that you have so that you may get more light by doing what you should do, to take the step you see before you with what light you have, and when you see another step, to take that, and then the next, and then the next.

Is it not also reasonable and necessary to openly confess this intention? *None of us liveth to himself* (Romans 14:7). We touch the lives around us. Those who are alone are set in families, and people are framed in one great network of society – even in one great organism of society, so that if one member suffers, all the members suffer with it, and if one member is healthful, it will help to impart health to all the rest. Your neighbor, your wife, your child, your business associate, and all the people who know you and look upon you have a right to know that as for you, you intend to do right as far as it will be shown unto you.

I never saw anyone who did these three things without coming to a knowledge of sin, to a knowledge of

God, to a knowledge of God's salvation, and to peace and light and hope and likeness unto Jesus Christ.

THEORETICAL AND PRACTICAL

There are two ways to investigate a machine. There are two ways to learn about anything. The one way is theoretical, and the other is practical. Some time ago, I was in a large carpet factory, and the proprietor, Mr. B., was showing us through the establishment. We went into a room that was a sort of inventor's room, and he said: "Here's a machine that I have just invented for making a new kind of carpet." There it was, towering up perhaps ten feet above the floor, and as large around as three or four men might reach with their hands touching, and with, I should say, a thousand needles, and a very great number of intricate parts. Mr. B. described it, and said, "This is this, and that is that, and the other is the other thing."

I tried to look wise for a while, but finally broke down and said, "You might as well talk Choctaw as to tell me all that. I will take your word that it makes carpet, but I am afraid that I do not have a mechanical mind, and I am sure that I could not understand how that machine can make carpet."

He said, "If you will stay here twenty-four hours, I will guarantee that you will understand it as well as I do."

I said, "You do not know the person whom you have undertaken to teach. I am sure there is nothing on earth that could show me how that machine can make carpet, even if I should stand here for the next twenty-four years."

"Come here," he said, and he took me into another room where he had one of the machines in motion, and I saw it make the carpet. Then I knew that it did it, just as well as if I could have uttered all those mysterious words, and I understood everything about every portion of that machine.

Now there are two ways to know the salvation of Christ. One of them would be just as impossible for you to understand as it would have been for me to understand the explanation given to me about that machine. To know all about God would take an infinite mind, one that could reach into all space and all time and understand all history and all prophecy and all mystery. In order to know all about God,

In order to know all about God, you would have to be God Himself.

you would have to be God Himself. You would have to have more time and a greater brain and a longer development and culture than anyone in the world. It is a theoretical thing that someone would do that, but it is not an attainable or practical thing.

However, there is another way to know God. Set the machine in motion and see what it will do. Begin to obey God. Act as though the Word of God means what it says when it says that *he became the author of eternal salvation unto all them that obey him* (Hebrews 5:9). Begin to do His will and see if you will not know of the doctrine. As you go, you will be cleansed.

KNOWLEDGE OF SIN, AND SORROW FOR IT

I believe that such an effort as this will lead to four things. In the first place, it will lead to a knowledge of sin, and to sorrow for it. If all of the Bible is profitable for reproof and correction (2 Timothy 3:16), I believe that practice is even more so, and that anyone who strives to do the will of God will be convicted of sin. I believe that *godly sorrow worketh repentance to salvation not to be repented of* (2 Corinthians 7:10), and that godly sorrow comes to us in proportion as we are godly.

I have had more pain today for one hasty word that suddenly escaped my lips than I had on account of all the sins in my life while I was an unconverted man. I believe that the nearer we get to God, the more sensitive to sin we become, until the slightest sin will pain us, just as the smallest speck will pain the eye if it falls upon it.

When Paul was about enlisting in God's service, or shortly afterward, he said that he was not worthy to be called an apostle (1 Corinthians 15:9). Then he said he was *less than the least of all saints* (Ephesians 3:8). And at the time that he said he was ready to be offered, he also said he was the chief of sinners (1 Timothy 1:15). Now I do not believe that he was growing more wicked all the time, but I think he was realizing more and more what sin meant and was becoming more sensitive to the touch of sin.

You might be down in a dark cellar tonight with all sorts of loathsome things around you. The atmosphere might be filled with impurities, and some hideous, slimy reptile might come within half an inch of your hand or even your face, and you might not mind it because you did not see what was around you. But as the light came in and you began to realize these things, you would quickly move away from this crawling reptile, and you would try to stamp that loathsome thing out of existence. As the light grew brighter and brighter, at last you would see that the very air around you was filled with that which was poisonous and repulsive. It is the same way with someone who sets himself to do the will of God, as God shows it to him. Sin seems exceedingly sinful, and more and more sinful as he goes on with his diligent and sincere effort to do the will of God.

> Sin seems exceedingly sinful as a person goes on with his sincere effort to do the will of God.

I knew of a man who was known as "the man who had never wept." No one had ever seen tears upon his face. One night he was deeply convicted of sin in a meeting, and finally, with great trembling, he took hold of the seat in front of him, pulled himself up to a partially erect posture, and asked, "Can a man be saved who has never wept?" Even as he said it, he let go of the seat, fell back into the pew, and burst into tears. Oh, I believe that tears would come to cheeks that were not used to them if only some would be willing to do the will of God.

I knew of a man in the army who was said to be the wickedest man in the regiment. One night he attended the regimental prayer meeting, and he stood up and said very calmly, "Comrades, I am going to lead a godly life." The soldiers were surprised because they thought that a wicked man would have to manifest deeper concern about sin in order to get rid of it. He tried it for one day, and then he went to the prayer meeting the next night. This time he had concern enough. He could hardly speak. He said, "Comrades, I did not do right when I told you last night that I was going to lead a godly life. I don't know that God can forgive me. I have just received two letters that informed me of the death of two people. One of them was a young man who has just died of delirium tremens, from withdrawal of alcohol, at my home in New England. The other is a young woman who has died in a place of shame in Washington. I led them both astray! God, can there be mercy for a wretch like me?"

God did save that man, but until the day of his death, he was never heard to pray without saying, "O God, help me to do good enough to counterbalance the evil of my past life."

Oh, friends, you would have concern enough if only you would openly begin with what light you have to do the will of God.

SOLUTION OF DOUBTS

There is another thing that would come to you, and that is the solving of every doubt. I believe there is no unbeliever walking in the midst and labyrinth of doubt who would not see a clear road that would shine with light up to the portals of the City of God, if only he would be willing openly to do what God showed him that He wanted him to do. I believe there is no poor wretch sitting now in some loathsome place, bound hand and foot with the chains of some selfish or carnal or covetous vice, who would not find the chains broken and would rise up a free man if only he was willing to do the will of God.

There was a man in a New England city who was an unbeliever. He had forty-five young men, I think it was, associated with him in an infidel club, of which he was president. Some revival meetings were in progress in that city, and one day the pastor of the church where the meetings were being held met this man on the street and invited him to come to the meetings.

The man said, "I don't know that I should go, but I am one who professes to believe in morality, and I think these meetings are having a good moral influence on the community. They have my approval so far. I'll tell you what I would like. I would like to see some of my young men go to these meetings. To be honest with you, some of the young men in our society are getting pretty far away from the path they should walk in, and I suppose I am somewhat responsible for them. I would like to have them take any sort of a moral tonic that would fix them up."

The minister said, "Suppose you invite them to come."

"I am willing to ask them," was the reply.

The minister met him the next day and said, "Did you ask the young men to come to the meetings?"

"Yes, but none of them would go."

"Did you tell them you would come yourself?"

"No, I did not. I told them I would not go. If I would

go, people would say that there had been a radical change in me. It would cause a great deal of discussion, and my action would be misunderstood. I am sure I should not go."

The minister said, "I will tell you what I will do. If you will go see your young men, and tell them you are going to the meeting, and then let me know how many are coming with you, I will reserve a block of seats for you. Then, when you come and take them, I will tell the people that you have not come to the meeting because you have stopped being an infidel, but because you think that this is a good moral movement, and in that way you are willing to support it."

The infidel said, "If you will do that, I will come."

He came, and twenty-six of his young men were with him. They sat down in the block of reserved seats, and of course, the people all looked at them. The minister rose up and made the statement as he said he would. The meeting went on, and five of those young men were converted that night. The person who seemed happiest over it was this infidel leader. He did not know of anything else that would keep them from their sinful ways, and the weight of responsibility was beginning to press upon him very seriously. The next night the young men were there again, and some others with them, and several others decided for Christ.

As the days went by, the man most interested in getting the young men to rise and confess Christ was this infidel. He did not have to worry anymore about the young men going to saloons and gambling halls and places of evil repute. He began to be very much relieved, and he seemed very happy when one after another took a stand for Christ.

The last night of the meetings came. The people had gone out, and the pastor and one of the deacons were at the front of the church. This man came up and said to the pastor, "I have been so busy for the last two weeks that I have not had time to take stock of my thoughts at all, and I hardly know where I stand. But if you will see me tomorrow morning at eleven o'clock, I will come to your house and have a conversation with you to see whether there is any way by which I can renounce my unbelief and become a Christian."

The men both smiled, and the agnostic saw what the smile meant. He said, "You do not think that I am a Christian, do you?"

The minister said, "If you will go on as you are doing now, you will be one of the best Christians on earth."

He never went to talk with the minister about his soul. His doubts all disappeared that night. Every difficulty that had been in his way was removed. He stood up in the next meeting where he had an opportunity and made a confession of Jesus Christ. He gathered his young men into the Sunday school and became the teacher of a large Bible class. As he went, he was cleansed.

When Lady Henry Somerset was seeking God, she heard a voice say, "My child, if you will act as if I were, you will know that I am." She was *not disobedient unto the heavenly vision* (Acts 26:19), and she came into God's light.

I know at least a hundred other examples like these, and I will tell of one more. There was an unbelieving German professor from the University of Berlin who visited London. He was spending part of his time with Dr. R., the rector of one of the English churches. Dr. R. did not speak to him on religious topics until he had been there a week and was preparing to leave. One day, after the professor had attended a service in the church and they were together in the vestry, the pastor spoke to him about his spiritual welfare. The professor said, "I do not believe certain things about the Christian religion. I do not believe in Jesus Christ as the Son of God. I do not believe in the inspiration of the Bible or in miracles. I think there may be a God. In fact, I am inclined to think there is a God, but I do not think there is any way by which any one can get acquainted with Him."

The pastor said, "Professor, would you like to know that there is a God?"

He replied, "Yes, I would, but I do not think God has revealed Himself to men."

The pastor said, "Professor, do you think that if God were kindly disposed toward His creatures, and if there were a way in which He could reveal Himself to men, He would do it?"

The professor said, "Yes, I think if He were kindly disposed, and were able to do it, that He would. But I do not think that He can."

"Do you think He is kindly disposed toward His creatures?"

"I would have to believe that, or He would crush us out of existence or fill us with continual misery."

"Professor, if God would reveal Himself to you, would you be willing to meet the consequences and do what He told you to do if He would show you His will?"

"Yes, if God could do it, and would do it, I would do what He showed me. But I do not think that He can."

"Did you ever ask Him?"

"No, I have never felt that that would be consistent."

"Professor, will you reverently kneel with me here, and after I have prayed, will you say what you can honestly say out of your heart concerning your desire for God to reveal Himself to you?"

"Yes, I will."

They knelt down, and the minister prayed. Then the professor said, "O God, if you can hear what I say to You now, and if You can reveal Yourself to me, I pledge myself that I will do what You show me You want me to do."

They stayed on their knees for half an hour, and then suddenly, without any warning, the professor jumped to his feet and said, "I believe in Jesus Christ! I see it all, and it is glorious; it is glorious!"

He went back to Germany and became as a center of blazing light, illuminating the region round about. As he went, he was cleansed.

REMOVAL OF STUMBLING BLOCKS

Then, in the third place, this would lead to the removal of every stumbling block. *Great peace have they which love thy law*, said the psalmist, *and nothing shall offend them* (Psalm 119:165). That is, they will have no stumbling block.

Consider two things at which people stumble. For instance, consider the excuse that hypocrites in the church are keeping them out of it. I do not believe it is true that any hypocrite is keeping anyone who honestly wants to know God out of the church of Christ. But whether that is so or not, you can get over that difficulty. Begin to lead a godly life, and you will have all that you can do to take care of yourself. You will not be concerned about the hypocrites in the church, except to help them to become pure and righteous. There is no hypocrite in my way all the distance from the place where I stand up to the time when I will stand before God in the glory of His eternal kingdom. There is not a hypocrite in the way

> Begin to lead a godly life, and you will not be concerned about the hypocrites in the church.

of anyone who determines to do the will of God and wants to be like the Son of God, who was manifested upon earth. The hypocrites are all going the other way.

There are some people who say honestly that they are afraid they will not hold out. They say, "Suppose I would try it. What guarantee do I have that I will succeed?" If you were in Mr. Moody's home and asked him about a certain clock on the wall in the dining room, he would probably tell you a story. This clock was given to him by a lady in London who came to one of Mr. Moody's meetings. She was very angry at some things he said. She came back the next night, however, and was even angrier. She came back the next night, and her anger began to vanish. The night after that she was also there, and she became deeply convicted of sin.

The next night, she was in the inquiry meeting, and she came night after night until one night she said to Mr. Moody, "I realize that I am a sinner. I believe that Jesus Christ is the Son of God, but I believe that I cannot be a Christian. Whether it is my sin, or what it is, I do not know, but I do not believe that if I began to be a Christian, I could ever hold out."

Mr. Moody tried every way he could to get her to decide to try – but he failed, until he thought of that old story about the pendulum. On the first day of January, the pendulum began to count up what it had to do. It had to tick so many ticks in a minute, and there were so many minutes in an hour, and so many hours in a day, and so many days in a year, and it would likely have to keep on ticking for so many years. When it found out the millions of times it would have to tick, it said, "It's of no use; I will stop right now." Then this thought occurred to the pendulum: "It is only one tick at a time." So it began to tick, and it ticked the next tick, and the next, and the next, and it is still ticking.

This lady said to Mr. Moody, "I will tick the first tick now," and she is still ticking for Christ. She gave that clock to Mr. Moody. She is now one of the most earnest Christians in the city of London. She asked him, if anyone would refer to that clock, to tell them the story – that it is only a tick at a time. Blessed be God, it is as simple as that! *As they went, they were cleansed* (Luke 17:14).

ASSURANCE

Now there is one thing more. Such a determined and sincere effort will lead to knowledge, assurance, confidence, peace, and joy. Here are two young men, John and James. John is a fine boy. He is very industrious, very studious, and very happy. James is a miserable, contemptible loafer, and he thinks, "I wonder if I can be as happy as John. I am miserable all the time, but there is John. He works twice as hard as I do, and he is happy all the time. I will see if I can be happy. I will imitate John."

He notices that John gets up at six o'clock in the morning and chops a lot of kindling for his mother. Then he brings in the water and helps her in other ways, spends some time studying, and then goes off to school and applies himself to his lessons and recites them well. So the next morning, James gets up at six o'clock. It is pretty difficult for him. He rubs his eyes, gets dressed, and then goes down and splits the wood. He finds that even more difficult.

Then he goes off to school and tries to learn his lessons, but he finally falls asleep, and the teacher wakes him up in a way that is not pleasant. He says, "It's no use. I am different from John. I cannot do this sort of thing. I cannot be happy no matter how I try."

Suppose, though, that he tried it differently. Suppose he said, "I am a miserable, contemptible loafer. There is my good industrious brother, and I am going to be good." Suppose he attempts to do right, not because he wants to be happy, but because he wants to be good. He will find pretty soon that the same flow of satisfaction that John has will break out over him, and as he goes, he will be filled with peace.

It is the same way in the service of God. Do not try to be happy while you are spiritually sick. Get well. Do not try to see how happy you can be while the disease stays around you, but get rid of the disease and know the joy of a strong, well man or woman in Jesus Christ. As you go, you will be cleansed.

Do not try to be happy while you are spiritually sick. Get well.

A man in this country who won a multitude of souls to Christ when he first confessed Christ was in utter darkness, and he stayed that way for three weeks. Yet all that time he was attempting to do the will of God and was openly confessing Him. The pastor invited those who wanted to join the church to meet the committee, and when the committee met, this man appeared before them and said, "Gentlemen, it is as black as night. It is dark in me, and dark all around me, but I have set myself to do the will of God."

They said to him, "Suppose it stays dark. What are you going to do?"

He replied, "I am going to do the best I can in serving Christ."

They said to him, "Come into the church."

The very second that he was baptized, as he came up from the water, the light of God broke in upon his soul. I believe he would have died in the darkness unless he had been willing to obey this command of Christ. As he went, he was cleansed.

I remember one afternoon in Newark, New Jersey, when I was preaching in a church that was completely filled. As I began the sermon, a lady came in with a drunken man whom she had found on the street. She brought him down the aisle, looking this way and that to find a seat, but there was no place where they could sit down until they came to the platform. There were some steps right in front of the pulpit, and they sat down there. During the sermon, I saw that the man was weeping, and the very second I asked, "Is there anyone here who wants to be free from sin?" he rose up and said, "I do! I do!"

After the meeting was over, my associate, Mr. Greenwood, took him into another room and kneeled down with him. The man said, "Lord, I give myself to You. O God, if you ever saved anybody, save me." He came out into the other room and said to me, "Mr. Mills, I have done the best I can. I have given myself to God. I am the weakest and most sinful man on earth, but I do believe God is going to save me."

I said, "Hallelujah! I believe it too."

I told the people about it in the sermon the next afternoon as an illustration, and I said, "I do not see that man here today, but I believe God has saved him." As I said it, a man raised up his hand in the audience, and then I saw that it was this same man. It was no wonder that I did not know him. Christ was manifest in his face where He had not been the day before. I said, "Stand up, my brother." He stood up, and a beautiful blush came over his face. He looked like a nobleman, and I said, "Do you want to say a word?"

He said, "Yesterday I was a wreck, and today I am a man." As he went, he was cleansed.

FINAL APPLICATION

Now for the final application. First of all, I speak to Christians. If you are not right in your experience, you are wrong in your life. If the Bible is a dull, dead book to you, if you do not know what it means to have God's peace, if you do not have strength in temptation, if you do not have power to win people to Christ, you are wrong in your life. If you fulfilled the conditions, you would be cleansed. If you are not cleansed, it is because you have not obeyed the plain voice of God. Oh, my brother, my sister, will you begin to obey God now? Give Him the last thing. As you do, you will be cleansed.

> If the Bible is a dull, dead book to you, if you do not know what it means to have God's peace, you are wrong in your life.

To you who have said that the Christian way was mysterious, let me say that it is the only simple thing in the world. You have said that you could not understand it. You can understand it better than you can understand how you breathe. It is the only thing that you can understand. If you will do the will of God, Jesus says you will know of the doctrine, and He will bring you into everlasting life. In the name of God, whom you and I will meet at the day of separation, I throw down this challenge and ask you to test it. Will you say here, clearly and openly, that you are willing to do the will of God? As you go, you will be cleansed.

Someone asked Samuel Taylor Coleridge if he could prove the truth of Christianity, and he said, "Yes. Try it." *Taste and see that the LORD is good* (Psalm 34:8). As you go, you will be cleansed.

A young woman left her home to go and see her pastor to ask him to point her to Christ. She was concerned about her sins and salvation. As she stepped on the streetcar, she met three of her closest friends. Something said to her, "Do not tell them where you are going," and something else said, "Tell them, and ask them to go with you." Eventually she went over and sat by them, and they asked her where she was going. She said, "Girls, I have made up my mind to be a Christian, and I am going to see our minister and ask him if he will show me how. I wish you would go with me." They declined to go, and she went alone.

She arrived at the minister's house and rang the bell. He came to the door himself, and she stood there hesitating a minute. Then she said, "Doctor, I started to come to see you to ask you to lead me to Christ, but now that I have come, I want to tell you that I have found Christ." As she went, she was cleansed.

Now, reader, are you willing to say that you will make an honest effort to do the will of God? Are you willing to say that as far as you receive the light, you will act up to the light?

Chapter 6

NAAMAN THE SYRIAN

By John McNeill

Now Naaman, captain of the host of the king of Syria, was a great man with his master, and honourable, because by him the LORD *had given deliverance unto Syria: he was also a mighty man in valour, but he was a leper. And the Syrians had gone out by companies, and had brought away captive out of the land of Israel a little maid; and she waited on Naaman's wife. And she said unto her mistress, Would God my lord were with the prophet that is in Samaria! for he would recover him of his leprosy. And one went in, and told his lord, saying, Thus and thus said the maid that is of the land of Israel. And the king of Syria said, Go to, go, and I will send a letter unto the king of Israel. And he departed, and took with him ten talents of silver, and six thousand pieces*

*of gold, and ten changes of raiment. And he
brought the letter to the king of Israel, saying, Now when this letter is come unto thee,
behold, I have therewith sent Naaman my
servant to thee, that thou mayest recover
him of his leprosy.*

*And it came to pass, when the king of Israel
had read the letter, that he rent his clothes,
and said, Am I God, to kill and to make
alive, that this man doth send unto me to
recover a man of his leprosy? wherefore
consider, I pray you, and see how he seeketh
a quarrel against me. And it was so, when
Elisha the man of God had heard that the
king of Israel had rent his clothes, that he
sent to the king, saying, Wherefore hast
thou rent thy clothes? let him come now
to me, and he shall know that there is a
prophet in Israel.*

*So Naaman came with his horses and with
his chariot, and stood at the door of the
house of Elisha. And Elisha sent a messenger unto him, saying, Go and wash in
Jordan seven times, and thy flesh shall
come again to thee, and thou shalt be clean.
But Naaman was wroth, and went away,
and said, Behold, I thought, He will surely
come out to me, and stand, and call on
the name of the* LORD *his God, and strike*

*his hand over the place, and recover the
leper. Are not Abana and Pharpar, rivers
of Damascus, better than all the waters
of Israel? May I not wash in them, and be
clean? So he turned and went away in a
rage.*

*And his servants came near, and spake unto
him, and said, My father, if the prophet had
bid thee do some great thing, wouldest thou
not have done it? how much rather then,
when he saith to thee, Wash, and be clean?
Then went he down, and dipped himself
seven times in Jordan, according to the saying of the man of God: and his flesh came
again like unto the flesh of a little child, and
he was clean.* – 2 Kings 5:1-14

LEPROSY, A TYPE OF SIN

Leprosy is a type of sin. How much teaching there is in
the type, you and I hardly know. When I preached once
on the cleansing of one of the New Testament lepers, I
said that I thought the sight of a leper would greatly tend
to awaken and give practical meaning in our minds to
all Bible teaching about the exceeding sinfulness of sin.
I have since seen a returned missionary who described
to me what leprosy really is and the awful effect that
the first acquaintance with it has upon one's eyes and
heart and understanding. The majority of people have
not seen it, but let us understand that leprosy is one

of the Bible's representatives of the intense malignity and defilement of the mortal disease that has attacked you and me: sin.

Naaman, then, was a typical man, a man afflicted and covered with this typical disease, and we have to follow the turnings and windings of the narrative in order to see how this typical sinner makes out when he comes into contact with the Lord God Almighty, the only God of grace and salvation for a leprous sinner.

THE DEPTH OF OUR NEED

Notice how the Bible puts this doctrine of the depth of our need as represented in the disease of leprosy. Many people stumble at it. The vision of a leper is a sermon to everyone who sees him as to what sin is in its insidious, but mortal and (except for one cure) incurable, ravages upon the inner man – the soul within us. I am stating the doctrine roughly and harshly. I may so put it in a way that you might think is a somewhat unbalanced way. Do not blame the Bible. The Bible is wonderfully considerate.

> The vision of a leper is a sermon to everyone who sees him as to what sin is.

As it states the case of Naaman, so it is willing to state the case of everyone. It states it, but see how softly it does so: *Now Naaman, captain of the host of the king of Syria* – it admits that he was a captain – *was a great man* – the Bible admits that he was great – *and honourable* – the Bible admits that – *because by him the* LORD *had given deliverance unto Syria* – he was quite a special man. *He was also a mighty man in valour* – a good general, perhaps the only general.

The Bible admits these things. However, after making these admissions and taking in everything by the way, it does say, and it dares to say, and it insists upon saying, *but he was a leper.*

Just as it is put there, so I would like to put it here. You are friendly. I admit that you are friendly. You are not a drunkard, or a harlot, or a degenerate. I am willing to admit that. However, at the bottom, the last analysis of all that you are yields this: you are a sinner; you are a leper. That is the last analysis. Taken into God's scales, tested in His crucibles, weighed in His balances, here is the analysis: *but he was a leper.* Friendly, but a friendly sinner. Refined, but a refined sinner. Wealthy, but a wealthy sinner. You may be a nobleman of the land, but you are a sinner in regard to your spiritual condition.

The Bible makes all allowances. It is not rude. It takes everything into consideration, but it will not speak false words. It will not say "peace" when there is no peace (Jeremiah 6:14; 8:11). It will not give you a clean bill and allow you to come into port when you should be riding quarantine because there is infectious disease on board. The Bible will be honest with you. While it makes all admissions, on certain grounds as to what differentiates you from other people who are dishonorable and dishonest and have broken vows outwardly, it goes straight into the conscience and says, "After all, you are a sinner. You are afflicted with an incurable disease that has no remedy except one, the knowledge and experience of which come not from earth, but straight and miraculously from heaven."

THE MEANS OF GRACE

And the Syrians had gone out by companies, and had brought away captive out of the land of Israel a little maid (1 Kings 5:2). Now does it not look as if this were a roundabout road to the well? After all this about Naaman, and who he was, and what was wrong with him, we are off to the Syrians.

What about them, and what about this little maid who waited on Naaman's wife? Out of little events come great events. Large doors turn upon small hinges. Such a thing as this wonderful story of God's gracious dealing with poor Naaman turns upon that seemingly trivial incident that a marauding, thieving band of Syrians took away captive this little maid when they crossed the borders and went into Israel. They "builded better then they knew." I can imagine that the band of Syrians came back, and all their plunder was a little maid.

Oh, how their companions laughed at them! It seemed to have been a poor excursion, a great deal of toil and trouble and effort for very little, when they came back with only this little girl. *Who hath despised the day of small things?* (Zechariah 4:10). No wise man has done so. Fools do it every day. Do not despise little folk. Do not despise small things. Do not despise the day of little things. What a great work this little maid did! She has found for herself a prominent place in the picture gallery of God's Word. She will be exhibited to all eternity.

Were there not kings and queens and mighty men who shined and blazed and paraded for a little while, and then went down to a dusty death? Their names and their memorials have perished with them. But that little girl, a stranger in a strange land, away there in Syria, lives forever in the imperishable record of the Word of God.

She waited on Naaman's wife. And she said unto her mistress, Would God my lord were with the prophet that is in Samaria! For he would recover him of his leprosy. And one went in, and told his lord, saying, Thus and thus said the maid that is of the land of Israel (2 Kings 5:2-4). What a simple testimony she bore, but what a splendid preacher she was! She had all the qualifications of a first-rate, successful preacher. She had a message, and she spoke it simply, directly, and with great assurance. She spoke what she knew. There was a ring of sincerity and convic-

> God has chosen the weak things, the lowly things, things that are despised, to do His work.

tion in what she said, and it affected her mistress. May God grant that my words may affect somebody now!

THE SIMPLE GOSPEL

Now the same thing is still working in and through the gospel. On the surface, it seems to be a weak, foolish, despised, and despicable thing – the word of a simple girl against all the misery and damaging power of leprosy. But God has chosen the weak things, the lowly things, things that are despised, to do His work, to bring to nothing things that are, to save souls, to give to Him eternal fame and honor.

Do we know this gospel? Do we know the prophet who is in Israel – no longer Elisha, but the Lord Jesus Christ, the Prophet of prophets, the King and Lord and Head of them all, the incarnation and embodiment of all healing power and spiritual virtue?

Then if we know Him, let us not only know Him in our hearts, but let us simply and sincerely testify for Him, and He will spread our testimony on the wings of the wind and make it tell as He did with this little girl: *One went in, and told his lord* (2 Kings 5:4). The king of Syria wrote to the king of Israel. Crowns sometimes fall upon very unworthy heads. Both of these kings seem to be very sorry figures, do they not? The king of Syria was going to do it all, and he said, *Go to, go, and I will send a letter unto the king of Israel. And [Naaman] departed, and took with him ten talents of silver, and six thousand pieces of gold, and ten changes of raiment* (2 Kings 5:5). How this poor girl's little simple gospel is being spoiled! Did she say a single word about kings, or about talents of silver, or about changes of raiment? Then see how they have corrupted the simplicity of her simple testimony.

What did they make of it? *He brought the letter to the king of Israel, saying, Now when this letter is come unto thee, behold, I have therewith sent Naaman my servant to thee, that thou mayst recover him of his leprosy. And it came to pass, when the king of Israel had read the letter, that he rent his clothes, and said, Am I*

God, to kill and to make alive, that this man doth send unto me to recover a man of his leprosy? (2 Kings 5:6-7).

There are some things that kings and councils and parliaments cannot do. This is one of them. They are completely at their wits' end, and God will not give this glory except in one way, and this blessing except along a particular line. One thing does come out of it clearly, and that is the emphasizing of the point with which I began. Leprosy evidently was regarded as incurable. *Am I God, to kill and to make alive, that this man doth send unto me to recover a man of his leprosy? Wherefore consider, I pray you, and see how he seeketh a quarrel against me* (2 Kings 5:7).

> Where is all the power of kings and lords and princes and councils to save a sinner?

Oh, that we had the same understanding today about sin! Oh, that men and women were revived to a simple and intense conviction that sin is incurable, and that there is no remedy except the heavenly, the supernatural! Where is the wise man's wisdom? Where is all the power of kings and lords and princes and councils to save a sinner? It is reduced to utter contempt.

THE POWER OF GOD

And it was so, when Elisha the man of God had heard that the king of Israel had rent his clothes, that he sent to the king, saying, Wherefore hast thou rent thy clothes? Let him come now to me, and he shall know that there is a prophet in Israel (2 Kings 5:8). Does not that look a little like boasting at first? *Let him come to me.* Yes, it is boasting, but it is boasting in the right way. When a man boasts in God, *the humble shall hear thereof, and be glad* (Psalm 34:2).

The meek hear of a testimony like this, and instead of being offended at it and calling it vainglory, they glory in it, for Elisha is not lifting up himself here, but is lifting up the God who gave him all the power that he had. Let us challenge the world's need and the world's problem. Let us call upon men and women to come and look our way and give us a test.

You ran here and there and everywhere to get rid of your leprosy. Do you now have peace in your soul and power and strength? Then if not, will you finally come to us? In myself, I am poor and weak and vile and nothing, but I dare to say that I preach a gospel that could change every sinner as mightily as Naaman was changed after Elisha had finished with him. Oh, that God would revive preachers in a simple faith in the message they have to deliver!

After all, things are very sad now. There is dreadful trouble in the land, a terrible problem, and we cannot solve it. The power of the state, the power of the world's wisdom, and the power of the world's deepest sympathy seem to make no more impression on it than the king's advice and the king's sympathy made upon the sickness of his beloved general. But there is still balm in Gilead (Jeremiah 8:22). The problem is not as hopeless as we think, and the distress is not as dreadful, for there is one voice rising sharp and clear above the clanging voices of a thousand counselors who are darkening counsel by words without knowledge (Job 38:2). And this is the voice: *Believe on the Lord Jesus Christ, and thou shalt be saved, and thy house* (Acts 16:31). It is a message straight from Jesus Christ, who died and rose again.

So Naaman came with his horses – they were not lepers, but he brought them – *and with his chariot, and stood at the door of the house of Elisha* (2 Kings 5:9). Now, Elisha, here is your test. You were never in such a perilous place before, after all that has been said about Israel and Israel's God. How people criticize the gospel! Will they eventually open their eyes? Will they at last cease from criticizing? Will they cease from wanting to pull themselves up on their own? Will they cease from striving and planning and trying, and will they accept the gospel as helpless lepers as they should do? As God is my witness, I do believe that if you have not been washed in the blood of Christ, Naaman's loathsomeness is only a poor picture of your condition in the sight of God.

No, Elisha was not being tested, nor was God; but Naaman was on trial, and he did not come through it very well at first. Elisha sent a messenger unto him, saying, *Go and wash in Jordan seven times, and thy flesh shall come again to thee, and thou shalt be clean. But Naaman was wroth and went away,* and you remember what he said: *Behold, I thought, He will surely come out to me* (2 Kings 5:10-11). *To me.* "Yes, I am a leper, but I am not an ordinary leper. I am a general, a prince. I am here with these jingling horses and chariots. Will he deal with me in this way?"

Have you never experienced this rage? Is it not in your veins at this moment? After all, the worst kind of a gospel hearer is that one who comes and goes, and comes and goes, and you never find him either sad, or glad, or mad – never. There they are, like a ditch without fall or flood – like the Mediterranean without ebb or flow, but at the one fall-less and floodless contemptible level. I like to see people mad in a certain way. When a man like Naaman is being led along a line like this – when he is taken so far away out of his own sphere, or so far off the beaten track, so completely away from what he expects, when the Lord's message through Elisha falls upon him at an angle of incidence so unexpected – I can quite understand him. I cannot suppose that the Lord was angry, and I do not suppose that Elisha was angry. They completely understood it. They knew exactly what the effect would be.

When people are awakened from a deep sleep, and awakened in a hurry because there is something urgent and imminent, they often wake up annoyed and irritable; they even wake up angry. I suppose that if I came to you tomorrow morning with all your friendliness and sweetness and gentleness, and seized you by the hand, put my hand on your shoulder, and shook you rudely and woke you up, when you arose you would not have all your "Polite Letter Writer" phrases just ready at the time. You would likely be a little irritated, and you would likely think that I was very inconsiderate. But if in the midst of all your annoyance and anger I showed you that I had a just cause for what I had done, and that there was a fire, and that the fire was not in the next street or even in the next house, but was in your own house, I think when you realized that, you would thank me, and you would say that if I had been polite and had awakened you gently and calmly, I would not have been your friend.

So it is with the gospel preachers, and so it was with Elisha. Poor Naaman was far gone, and what he needed was quick medicine. He needed something that went straight to the point. I admit that there was seeming rudeness in the wording. I agree that there was superiority, for when God speaks, you must allow Him to be superior and imperial; never forget that. The gospel does plead, but in it all and through it all, the gospel is a command, and you disobey it at the risk of eternal damnation. Believe, repent, go work, and go as quickly as you can; that is the gospel. It is a command, and it is in your interest, sinner, that the gospel is on the surface seemingly rude and inconsiderate and unjust.

> The gospel is a command, and you disobey it at the risk of eternal damnation.

THE LEPROSY OF PRIDE

Naaman was angry and said, *I thought.* That is what is wrong with most of us. Why are you not a happy Christian? I will tell you in a word. You are troubled with the same disease that Naaman had. Leprosy was his trouble outwardly, and the leprosy of pride was his trouble inwardly. He needed to be humbled before he could be healed.

Your pride is very likely intellectual pride, intellectual vanity, intellectual conceit. You juggle with the names of Huxley and Spencer and Darwin, and you want to impress and overawe the poor preacher with a sense of your opinion. You say, "When I go to hear a sermon, I think and I wish and I like . . ." And when you do not get what you like, the preacher gets your most disagreeable verdict.

Now, my dear friend, come away from that, if you will. You are a poor, helpless, hopeless, condemned sinner. Until you receive the gospel in childlike simplicity, you cannot be saved. You are neither fit to live, nor fit to die, and you have to do both, so come down off your horse of pride and cleverness and pretentiousness and self-conceit. Forget your wisdom and forget your knowledge, and remember that in all past ages, and even in this century, thanks to God, wise and educated men who have forgotten more about literature and science and philosophy than you ever learned have, with all their knowledge, labored to be as simple, genuine, evangelical believers in the blood of the Lamb as any who ever lived.

You *thought*. Thank you for nothing. What did you think? Let us hear it. Well here it is: *I thought, He will surely come out to me, and stand, and call on the name of the LORD his God, and wave his hand over the place, and recover the leper* (2 Kings 5:11). That is, "I thought that he was a magician and an enchanter, and that he would come and say, 'Hey! Presto! Pass!' and the thing would be done." Is not that about the length and breadth and depth and height, my friend, of your idea of what genuine religion is?

The thoughts of people in Naaman's condition are worth little! Naaman spoke out his thought, and there it is. When salvation comes to us, it comes when we get rid of our own thought, or we hold in our own thought, whatever it may be, and we choke it down, and we allow God to speak. God's thoughts are what we need to know, and God says, *My thoughts are not your thoughts, neither are your ways my ways, saith the* LORD. *For as the heavens are higher than the earth, so are my ways higher than your ways, and my thoughts than your thoughts* (Isaiah 55:8-9). Be silent, be still, and know that God is here – that God is speaking, and that you should bow your head, keep silent, and believe!

Are not Abana and Pharpar rivers of Damascus, better . . . ? (2 Kings 5:12). Oh, yes! With what contempt people sometimes speak of the gospel until they have tried it.

THE OLD GOSPEL

Naaman, dear, if Abana and Pharpar were waters that would have cleansed you, why did you not go to them? Why did you come here at all? Have not some of us spoken in the same rude and contemptuous way about what we call old, narrow-minded, bigoted, Puritanical doctrines – until we tried them? But when the day came when our sins were clinging to us, the sorrows of death compassed us, and the gates of hell got hold upon us and we found trouble and sorrow, then we changed our tune. When we were content and well, we could speak contemptuously about the old gospel and call this salvation by blood a doctrine of the slaughterhouse. However, when we stand naked and shivering and ready to perish, then this old gospel of the cross, the gospel of salvation through the doing and dying of another, is to us like the sound of heaven's own music. Do not talk against the gospel, my friend. You are only showing your lack of heart or the depth of your ignorance.

And his servants came near, and spake unto him, and said, If the prophet had bid thee do some great thing, wouldest thou not have done it? How much rather then, when he said to thee, Wash, and be clean? Then he went down, and dipped himself seven times in Jordan (2 Kings 5:13-14). The man of God had told Naaman, *Go and wash in Jordan seven times.* Naaman had to humble himself to obey the gospel, and you and I must do the same. We do not give up intellectuality and the powers of the mind. We simply crucify their pride, that is all.

BLESSING COMES BY OBEDIENCE

And his flesh came again like unto the flesh of a little child, and he was clean (2 Kings 5:14). This is the gospel. Will you try it? Will you do, my friend, what you never did before? Will you humble yourself simply to believe? The gospel will never prove its power in anybody as long as the person criticizes and questions. The gospel is for believing; the gospel is for receiving. *O taste and see that the LORD is good: blessed is the man that trusteth in him* (Psalm 34:8).

At last, Naaman is a sadder and a wiser man. He is spoken to kindly by his servant. Naaman had his good points about him, but after those good points, there was the leprosy. There was no arguing against that. There was this sentence of death eating into him.

It is the same with you. While you are criticizing, you are dying. Hell opens its mouth to receive you while you are criticizing and wanting another gospel to satisfy you. Do not forget that. It is not for beggars to be choosers, and you are an absolute beggar at heaven's gate. You are completely dependent upon God's abundance and generosity, and when it is offered to you, it is not right for you to take the sneering or angry tone that you do. Let us cease from all such *superfluity of naughtiness* (James 1:21), and in simplicity, like the poor, dying lepers that we are, let us receive salvation through Jesus Christ, through His atonement.

> You are completely dependent upon God's abundance and generosity.

That dark, muddy Jordan was not a nice stream. It was really a very poor river from an artistic point of view, but it was in Israel. It was an Israelitish river, and away to it Naaman must go, even though he was a great man. So he went. He swallowed down his pride. He very likely said to himself, "Well, that servant of mine is true. He is right. I am a leper, and of course I am dying. I may as well try it. It would be a pity to come all this distance, with all these clanging horses and chariots, and go home and admit that I had come on a fool's errand. Maybe there is something in it after all."

So he went down. He "stooped to conquer,"[9] and he

---

9   *She Stoops to Conquer* is the title of a play that was written by Oliver Goldsmith. It was first performed in London in 1773.

conquered by stooping. He gave in to God, and he won. For a time, he seemed to be no better, only much wetter. But dipping seven times, when he came up the seventh time, he left his leprosy in the last plunge. The flesh came to him as with that leper in the New Testament to whom Christ said, *Be thou clean*, and immediately he was made whole (Matthew 8:3). As the poet says:

> He took a little water in his hand
> And laid it on his brow, and said, "Be clean!"
> And lo! the scales fell from him, and his blood
> Coursed with delicious coolness through his veins,
> And his dry palms grew moist, and on his brow
> The dewy softness of an infant's stole.
> His leprosy was cleansed, and he fell down
> Prostrate at Jesus' feet, and worshipped him.[10]

This is the gospel for lepers, Old Testament and New. Come near to the cleansing fountain, and in absolute humble simplicity, plunge into it.

> There is a fountain filled with blood
>   Drawn from Emmanuel's veins;
> And sinners plunged beneath that flood
>   Lose all their guilty stains.[11]

I have read a book or two. I hope I know a little about philosophy. I trust I know a little about science. I went

---

10 This is from the poem "The Leper," by Nathaniel Parker Willis (1806-1867).

11 This is a stanza from a hymn by William Cowper (1731-1800) that begins with "There is a fountain filled with blood."

for eight winters to a college and a divinity hall, and I was lectured and taught by the most cultured and eminent men of the day. But if tomorrow I am upon my deathbed, and if you want to come and give me a parting word, come, and I will tell you before you come what you may say. Do not mention this current century. Do not mention these "new gospels," which are no gospels. If you have no word, and if you have no text, that old hymn that I have just quoted will do, and especially the verse that I am going to quote now:

> The dying thief rejoiced to see
>> That fountain in his day:
> And there may I, though vile as he,
>> Wash all my sins away.

Ah, my child, you may despise this old gospel, but your mother died rejoicing in it. So did your father. If you are ever to see them and meet with them, if you are ever to sit down with the truly refined people, you must be washed in the blood of the Lamb. May the Lord, the Spirit, graciously plead His own cause, and may all of us come to the simplicity of faith in Jesus Christ, who died for our sins and rose again for our justification!

May all of us come to the simplicity of faith in Jesus Christ.

Chapter 7

OBEDIENCE

By Dwight L. Moody

And being made perfect, he became the author of eternal salvation unto all them that obey him. – Hebrews 5:9

M y subject is one that you will not like very well, but I found out a long time ago that the medicine we don't like is the best medicine for us. If there is anything that throws a coldness over a meeting, it is to talk about obedience. You can talk about love and heaven and other things, and people get so warmed that they shout; but when you talk about obedience, there is a sort of coldness over the meeting.

It is like a man I heard of who was preaching with great power. His employer heard of it and said, "I understand you are preaching, and they tell me you preach with great power."

"Yes," said the employee.

"Well, now," said the employer, "I will give you all the time you want to preach here, but you prepare a sermon on the Ten Commandments and preach on them, and emphasize the one on stealing, for there is a great deal of stealing by the employees here."

The man's countenance fell at once. He said he wouldn't like to do that. There wasn't the warmth in it that there was in some things. I have always noticed when you come right down to such matters that people don't like to be told about them because it comes a little too near home.

I once heard about a young minister who took the place of an old pastor, and he began to bear down pretty hard upon the sins of the people. A man came to him afterward and said, "Look here, young man, if you expect to keep this pulpit, you have got to stop that kind of preaching, for the people won't stand for it." There are a good many people who are delighted when you talk about the sins of the patriarchs and the sins of other Bible characters, but when you touch upon the sins of today, that is another thing. They say, "I don't like his style." They don't like his subject matter either, and perhaps you won't like this subject of obedience.

We are told that without faith it is impossible to please God (Hebrews 11:6), and you will find that it is impossible to please God without obedience. Your faith doesn't amount to much without obedience. *And being made perfect, he became the author of eternal salvation unto all them that obey him.* He gives eternal salvation unto all those who obey Him – not to all those who feel Him, or talk to Him, or who say, *Lord, Lord* (Matthew 7:21), but to those who obey Him. Eternal salvation means eternal safety.

EVERYTHING EXCEPT THE HEART OF MAN OBEYS GOD

Did you ever notice that everything except the heart of man obeys God? If you look right through history, you will find that this is true. In the beginning, *God said, Let there be light: and there was light* (Genesis 1:3). *Let the waters bring forth*, and the water brought forth abundantly (Genesis 1:20).

One of the proofs that Jesus Christ is God is that He spoke to nature, and nature obeyed Him. At one time He spoke to the sea, and the sea recognized and obeyed Him (Mark 4:39). He spoke to the fig tree, and instantly it withered and died (Matthew 21:19). It obeyed literally and immediately. He spoke to devils, and the devils fled (e.g., Matthew 8:16). He spoke to the grave, and the grave obeyed Him and gave back its dead (John 11:43-44).

When Jesus speaks to man, man will not obey Him. That is why man is out of harmony with God.

However, when He speaks to man, man will not obey Him. That is why man is out of harmony with God, and it will never be different until people learn to obey God. God wants obedience, and He will have it, or else there will be no harmony. In the first epistle of John, we read, *And the world passeth away, and the lust thereof: but he that doeth the will of God abideth for ever* (1 John 2:17). He says in another place that if we keep His sayings, we will never die (John 8:51). The world is like a floating island, and as securely as we anchor to it, we will be carried away by it.

NEAR TO GOD

If you want to get near God, just obey Him. That is the quickest way to get near Him. He takes those who obey Him into the nearest communion with Himself. Once while Jesus talked to the people, *behold, His mother and His brethren stood without, desiring to speak with him. Then one said unto him, Behold, thy mother and thy brethren stand without, desiring to speak with thee. But he answered and said unto him that told him, "Who is my mother? and who are my brethren?" And he stretched forth his hand toward his disciples, and said, "Behold my mother and my brethren! For whosoever shall do the will of my Father which is in heaven, the same is my brother, and sister, and mother"* (Matthew 12:46-50).

There is no friendship without obedience. The truest sign that we love God is that we obey Him. "I do love God," a little girl said to her father one day when he was speaking to her about loving God.

"Perhaps you think you do, dear," said the father.

"But I do."

"Suppose you would come to me and say, 'Papa, I love you,' and then run off and disobey me. Could I believe you?"

The child said, "No."

"Well," continued the father, "how can I believe that you love God when I see you every day doing things that He forbids?"

If ye love me, keep my commandments (John 14:15). It isn't a matter of feeling or picking out things we like to do, but it is doing what He commands us to do. Notice that Adam lost everything by disobedience, and the second Adam gained everything by obedience. *For as by one man's disobedience many were made sinners, so by the obedience of one shall many be made righteous* (Romans 5:19).

TO OBEY IS BETTER THAN SACRIFICE

Let me call your attention to another portion of Scripture: *And Samuel said, Hath the LORD as great delight in burnt offerings and sacrifices, as in obeying the voice of the LORD? Behold, to obey is better than sacrifice, and to hearken than the fat of rams* (1 Samuel 15:22).

God doesn't want sacrifice if there is disobedience. If we are living in disobedience to God, that is no sacrifice, but it is sacrilege. If Adam and Eve had obeyed God, there would have been no need of sacrifices of any kind. Many people want to bring Him a sacrifice instead of obeying Him. What does your work of charity amount to if you are not obedient? Do you think that you can gain heaven by sacrificing your money or your time? *To obey is better than sacrifice.*

Suppose a father sends his boy to school and he does not go. He says, "I don't want to go to school," and he goes off and fishes all day. He knows his father is very fond of trout. He says, "I know I have been disobedient, but I can sell these trout for fifty cents, and I will just take them home to my father. It will be a great sacrifice, but it will please my father." Do you think that will please him? Not at all. He wants obedience, and until his son obeys, his sacrifice is an abomination. The sacrifices of the wicked are an abomination to God and man (Proverbs 15:8). Don't let anyone deceive himself and think he is going to please God by giving something to Him when he is living in disobedience.

People say to me, "You talk against that gambler, but he is very good to the poor," and they think he is going to go to heaven because he is good to the poor. They say that God will have to remember him. My dear friend, as long as he is living a disobedient life, he cannot do a thing to please God. That boy cannot please his father until he is willing to obey and do the very thing he was told to do. It is much easier to bring a lamb or bullock to the altar than it is to bring ourselves. Do you know it?

> As long as that gambler is living a disobedient life, he cannot do a thing to please God.

I remember hearing a story about an Indian who wanted to come to the Lord. He brought his blanket, but the Lord wouldn't have it. He brought his gun, his dog, and his bow and arrow, but the Lord wouldn't have them. At last he brought himself, and the Lord took him. The Lord wanted *him*. What the Lord wants is not what you have got, but yourself, and you cannot do a thing to please God until you surrender yourself to Him.

Take the two Sauls. They lived about a thousand years apart. One started out well and ended poorly, and the other started out poorly and ended well. The first Saul got a kingdom and a crown. He had a lovely family (no father ever had a better son than Saul had in Jonathan). He had the friendship of Samuel, the best prophet there was on the face of the earth. Yet he lost the friendship of Samuel, he lost his crown, he lost his kingdom, and he lost his life – all through an act of disobedience. God took the crown from his head and put another man in his place. Why? Because he disobeyed. All his kingly dignity and power could not excuse him.

Now take the Saul of the New Testament. When God called him, he *was not disobedient unto the heavenly vision* (Acts 26:19), and he was given a heavenly kingdom. There was one act of obedience and one act of disobedience. The act of obedience gained everything, and the act of disobedience lost everything.

You will find that this is taking place constantly right through the Scriptures. I believe the wretchedness and misery and woe in our American cities today comes from disobedience to God. If we won't obey God as a nation, let us begin individually. Let us make up our minds that we will do it, no matter what it costs us, and we will have peace and joy.

A BLESSING OR A CURSE

In the book of Deuteronomy, we read, *Behold, I set before you this day a blessing and a curse; a blessing, if ye obey the commandments of the* LORD *your God, which I command you this day; and a curse, if ye will not obey the commandments of the* LORD *your God, but turn aside out of the way which I command you this day, to go after other gods, which ye have not known* (Deuteronomy 11:26-28). Isn't that enforced? Isn't the blessing of God resting upon a person who serves God? There is great reward in keeping God's laws and statutes (Psalm 19:11), but a great curse upon those who disobey God.

A lawyer once gave a client instructions of what to do, but the client did not follow the instructions, and he lost his case. He complained to his lawyer, who responded, "Well, you did not do what I told you."

Look at the wives and mothers who have gone right against the law of God and married ungodly men and drunkards. See what hells they are living in today! Just one act of disobedience. They are suffering tortures day by day, dying by inches. The whole country is more or less cursed by this disobedience.

A mother up in Minnesota told me that she had a little child who took a book and threw it out of the window. She told him to go and pick it up. The little boy said, "I won't."

She said, "What?"

He said again, "I won't."

She said, "You will. You go and pick up that book."

He said he couldn't do it. She took him outside and she waited for him to pick up the book. Dinner time came, and he hadn't picked up the book. She took him to dinner, and after it was over, she took him outside again. They sat there until teatime. When teatime came, she took him in and gave him his supper, and then took him outside and kept him there until bedtime. The next morning, she went out again and kept him there until dinnertime. He realized that he was in for a life job, so he picked up the book. She said she never had any trouble with the child afterward. Mothers, if you don't make your boy obey when he is young, he will break your heart later.

You say, "Cannot God make a person obey?" I suppose He could, but He does not work that way. He isn't going to force you against your will. He is going to draw you by the cords of love (Hosea 11:4), but if you are not going to obey Him, then you are going to suffer.

> God made man neither obedient nor disobedient, and a person must choose for himself.

God made man neither obedient nor disobedient, and a person must choose for himself. As Dr. Parker says, "A child can treat God with sulkiness and silence. The tiniest knee can stiffen and refuse to bow before Him."

Strive to enter in at the strait gate (Luke 13:24).
  "I will not."

Look unto me, and be ye saved (Isaiah 45:22).
  "I will not."

Come unto me, . . . and I will give you rest (Matthew 11:28).
  "I will not."

Seek ye first the kingdom of God (Matthew 6:33).
  "I will not."

Repent (Matthew 4:17).
  "I will not."

Turn ye, turn ye, . . . for why will ye die? (Ezekiel 33:11).
  "I will not."

Follow me (Matthew 4:19).
  "I will not."

Believe on the Lord Jesus Christ (Acts 16:31).
  "I will not."

Give me thine heart (Proverbs 23:26).
  "I will not."

Go work to day in my vineyard (Matthew 21:28).
  "I will not."

Remember the sabbath day, to keep it holy (Exodus 20:8).
  "I will not."

Lay up for yourselves treasures in heaven (Matthew 6:20).
  "I will not."

So we could go through the entire Bible, and we would
find that rebellious man refuses to obey God's commandments, but instead follows the devices and desires

of his own heart. God made man for His glory, but man joined the devil and became a rebel.

Now this is the question to be settled. The battle is fought on that one word of the will. The door hangs on that one hinge of the will. Will you obey? That is the question. Will you obey the voice of God and do as He commands you to do? No one can obey for you any more than anyone can eat and drink for you. You must eat and drink for yourself, and you must obey God for yourself.

> God requires literal, prompt, cheerful obedience. Nothing less will do.

God requires literal, prompt, cheerful obedience. Nothing less will do. If you changed the doctor's prescription only a little, you might turn it into strong poison. A Sunday school teacher once asked her class, "How is the will of God done in heaven?"

One child answered, "Cheerfully."

Another said, "By everybody."

A third responded, "All the time."

But the best answer was, "It is done without asking any questions."

DISOBEDIENCE BRINGS PUNISHMENT

People don't seem to think that there is anything in disobedience that needs to be punished. They shoot a soldier in the army for disobedience. As Alfred, Lord Tennyson wrote in "The Charge of the Light Brigade":

Theirs not to make reply,
Theirs not to reason why,
Theirs but to do and die.

It is said that an officer of engineers once told the Duke of Wellington that it was impossible to carry out some orders he had given. "Sir," replied the duke, "I did not ask your opinion. I gave you my orders, and I expect them to be obeyed." God never gave a command that we cannot obey. Perhaps we don't know the reason, but God knows it.

Will not the farmer be punished if he disobeys the laws of nature? Does not the same hold true in regard to spiritual laws? The only way to reap happiness in the life to come is to obey God's commandments in the life that now is.

People say, "Well, don't you think it is very unreasonable for God to punish Adam because he transgressed once?" Some years ago, a superintendent telegraphed to a man not to turn the bridge over a certain river until a special train passed. He waited and waited, and the man stood firm, until finally someone convinced him to open the bridge. He thought he would have time to let the boats pass and swing the bridge back before the train came. However, he had just got it opened when he heard the coming of the quick train. He did not have time to get the bridge back, and there was a tremendous accident and lives were lost.

The man went out of his mind and was sent to a madhouse, and his cry for years, until death released him, was, "If I only had! If I only had!" If he only had what? If he had only obeyed, those lives would not have been lost. In England, not long ago, a switchman just turned the switch at the wrong time, and twenty men were hurled into eternity, and a good many were maimed and hurt for life. He disobeyed just once.

SIMPLE OBEDIENCE

There is a story told about Stephen Girard, one of the first millionaires this country ever had. An Irishman had recently arrived in this country, and he had been walking around the streets of Philadelphia for a long time, unable to find any work. One day he went into Girard's office and asked him if he could give him something to do to keep soul and body together. Girard said, "Yes. Do you see that pile of bricks down there?"

"Yes."

"Well, pile it up at the other end of the yard."

The Irishman went to work. Night came on, and he had the work all done. He went into the office, touched his hat, got his pay, and asked if Mr. Girard had any work for him the next morning. Girard told him he had. The next morning, Girard said, "You go and carry that pile of bricks back to where you found it." The Irishman went at the work without a word. Night came on and he got his pay, and he asked if there would be work for him the next morning. Girard kept him marching up and down there for a number of days – until he saw that he was just the man he wanted.

One day he said, "You go down and bid that sugar off." When the auctioneer put the sugar up, here was an inexperienced Irishman bidding. The people laughed and made fun of him, and finally it was sold to him. The auctioneer said in a gruff tone, "Who is going to pay for this sugar?"

"Girard, sir."

"Are you Girard's agent?"

He was a mighty man then! Girard had found a man he could trust. God wants to find someone He can trust to obey Him.

BLESSED BY OBEDIENCE

Do you know that every person who was blessed while Christ was on earth was blessed in the act of obedience? Ten lepers came to Him, and He said, *Go show yourselves unto the priests* (Luke 17:14). They could have said, "What good is that going to do us? It was the priests who sent us away from our families." But they said nothing; and it came to pass that as they went, they were healed.

To know the truth and not to obey it is unprofitable.

Do you want to get rid of the leprosy of sin? Then obey God. You say you don't feel like it. Did you always feel like going to school when you were a child? Suppose a person only went to his business when he felt like it; he would fail in a few weeks.

Jesus said to another man, *Go, wash in the pool of Siloam* (John 9:7), and as he washed, he received his sight. He was blessed in the act of obedience. The prophet said to Naaman, *Go and wash in Jordan seven times* (2 Kings 5:10), and while he was dipping himself in the river, he was healed.

God wants simple obedience. You don't need to go to any theological seminary to find out how to obey, do you? Old Matthew Henry used to say, "If you live by the gospel precepts, you may live on the gospel promises." To know the truth and not to obey it is unprofitable. The Bible says more than fifty times that Moses did *as the LORD commanded him*. That was why Moses had the confidence of God.

ETERNAL SALVATION

If you want eternal salvation, you can have it now. The terms are right here. What are they? Obedience.

> *This is his commandment, that we should believe on the name of his Son, Jesus Christ* (1 John 3:23). *He that believeth on him is not condemned: but he that believeth not is condemned already, because he hath not believed in the name of the only begotten Son of God* (John 3:18).

If you disobey, you shut the only door of hope. You may make a profession of Christianity, you may join the church, and you may know the doctrine, but unless you listen to and obey God's commandments, it will all be of no avail.

Will you obey? You have got to settle this thing in your mind. Just make up your mind that you are going to obey. There is nothing very mysterious about it. You do not need to go to any old musty library to read up on obedience, do you? If God tells you to repent, then repent. This will be the greatest day you have ever seen if you make up your mind to obey Him. Will you do it?

Reader, decide now. In olden times, when a Roman ambassador came to a king who was not allied to the Empire, he said, "Will you have peace with Rome or not?" If the king asked for time to think it over, the ambassador used to draw a circle around the man with his rod and say, "You must decide before you step out of that circle; for if you do not say 'peace' before you cross the line, Rome will crush you with her armies."

Do not trespass any longer on God's mercy. *Choose you this day whom ye will serve* (Joshua 24:15).

This life will not last forever. The trumpet will one day sound and call you forth from your narrow bed. The graves will be opened, and you will be summoned forth to meet your God. The proud heart that rejects or mocks Christianity down here will be compelled to listen to the judgment sentence of God. The ears that will not obey the sound of the church-going bell will be compelled to obey the sound of the last trumpet. The eyes that behold evil here will one day gaze upon the spotless throne of God. Do not forever disobey. May God help you to submit your proud will without delay in loving, childlike obedience to Him.

Chapter 8

THE GLORIOUS GOSPEL

By T. De Witt Talmage

According to the glorious gospel of the blessed God, which was committed to my trust. – 1 Timothy 1:11

The greatest novelty of our time is the gospel. It is so old that it is new. As potters and artists are now attempting to fashion pictures and cups and unique items like those of nineteen hundred years ago, recently brought up from buried Pompeii (and such cups and pitchers and unique items are universally admired), so anyone who can uncover the real gospel from the mountains of stuff under which it has been buried will be able to present something that will attract the gaze, admiration, and adoption of all the people.

Amazing substitutes have been presented for what my text calls *the glorious gospel*. There are many people in this and all other large assemblies who have no more idea of what the gospel really is than they have of what is contained in the fourteenth chapter of "Zend-Avesta" of the Hindu scriptures. There is no philosophy about it. It is a plain matter of Bible statement and of child-like faith. The ablest theological professor is a Christian mother who, out of her own experience, can tell the four-year-old how beautiful Christ was on earth, how beautiful He now is in heaven, and how dearly He loves little children. Then she kneels down and puts one arm around the boy, and with her somewhat faded cheek against the rosy cheek of the little one, consecrates him for time and eternity to Him who said, *Suffer little children to come unto me* (Luke 18:16).

There sits the dear old theologian with his table piled up with all the great books on inspiration, exegesis, and apologetics for the Almighty. His little grandchild comes up to him for a good-night kiss and he accidentally knocks off the biggest book from the table, which falls on the head of the child, of whom Christ Himself said, *Out of the mouths of babes and sucklings thou hast perfected praise* (Matthew 21:16).

Ah, my friends, the Bible needs no apologetics. The throne of the last judgment needs no apologetics. Eternity needs no apologetics. Scientists may tell us that natural light is the "propagation of undulations in an elastic medium, and thus set in vibratory motion by the action of luminous bodies," but no one knows what gospel light is until his own blind eyes, by the touch of the divine Spirit, have opened to see the noonday of pardon and peace. Scientists may tell us that natural sound is "the effect of an impression made on the organs of hearing by an impulse of the air, caused by a collision of bodies, or by other means," but those only know what the gospel sound is who have heard the voice of Christ directly, say-

> Those only know what the gospel sound is who have heard the voice of Christ directly.

ing, *Thy sins are forgiven. . . . Thy faith hath saved thee; go in peace* (Luke 7:48, 50).

REGENERATION, NOT REFORM

Some people think that they can save the world by law and exposure of crime. From Portland, Maine, across to San Francisco, and back again to New Orleans and Savannah, many have gone into the detective business. By all means, that is worldly reform, but unless it is also gospel reform, it will be a dead failure. In New York, its main work has been to give us a change of leaders. We had a Democratic leader, and now it is to be a Republican leader, but the quarrel is who the Republican will be. Politics will never save the cities.

No reform will be successful and effective that does not begin with the heart. *A new heart also will I give you, and a new spirit will I put within you: and I will take away the stony heart out of your flesh, and I will give you an heart of flesh. And I will put my spirit within you, and cause you to walk in my statutes, and ye shall keep my judgments, and do them. . . . And ye shall be my people, and I will be your God* (Ezekiel 36:26-28).

Another class of people cover up the gospel with the theory that it makes no final difference what you believe or how you act. They say that everyone will go to heaven anyway. There they sit, side by side, in heaven: Garfield, and Guiteau who shot him; Lincoln, and John Wilkes Booth who assassinated him; Washington, and Thomas Paine who slandered him; Nana Sahib, and the missionaries whom he clubbed to death at Cawnpore; Herod, and the children whom he massacred; Paul, and Nero who beheaded him.

As a result of the promotion of such a mixed and blended heaven, there are millions of people in Christendom who expect to go straight to heaven from their immorality, drunkenness, and suicides, when among the loudest thunders that break over the basaltic island to which the apostle John was expatriated was the one in which God announced that *the abominable, and murderers, and whoremongers, and sorcerers, and idolaters, and all liars, shall have their place in the lake which burneth with fire and brimstone, which is the second death* (Revelation 21:8).

If the glorious gospel had been given full opportunity, I think that before this time the world would have had no need of pulpit, sermon, prayer, or church, but thanksgiving and hosannas would have resounded in the temple to which the mountains would have been pillars, the blue skies the dome, the rivers the baptistry, and all nations the worshippers in the auditorium of the outspread world. But so far from that, as I remarked in the opening sentence of this sermon, the greatest novelty of our time is the gospel. When the glorious gospel of the blessed God as spoken of in my text gets full swing, it will have a momentum and a power mightier than that of the Atlantic Ocean when, under the force of the September equinox, it strikes the Highlands of the Navesink.

GLORIOUS GOOD NEWS

The meaning of the word "gospel" is "good news," and my text says it is glorious good news. Therefore, we must tell it in our churches, over our dry-goods counters, in our factories, over our threshing machines, behind our plows, on our ships' decks, and in our homes, our nurseries, and our kitchens, as though it were glorious good news – and not with a boring tone in our voice and a dismal look on our faces as though Christianity were a rheumatic ache, a dyspeptic pain, a malarial chill, or an attack of nervous weakness.

Christ began His Sermon on the Mount with nine "blessed," or "happys,": *Blessed are the poor; blessed are they that mourn; blessed are the meek; blessed are they which do hunger and thirst after righteousness; blessed are the merciful; blessed are the pure in heart; blessed are the peacemakers; blessed are they which are persecuted for righteousness' sake; and blessed are ye, when men shall revile you* (Matthew 5:3-11). Blessed, blessed, blessed! Happy, happy, happy!

The gospel is glorious good news for the young since through Christ they may have their coming years honored, and for a lifetime, all the angels of God are to be their helpers and all the armies of heaven their allies! The gospel is glorious good news for the middle-aged since through Christ they may have their perplexities disentangled, their courage rallied, and their victory over all obstacles and hindrances made forever sure! This is glorious good news for the aged since they may have the sympathy of Him of whom the apostle John wrote, *His head and his hairs were white like wool, as white as snow* (Revelation 1:14), and the defense of the everlasting arms! The gospel is glorious good news for the dying since they may have ministering spirits to escort them, opening gates to receive them, a scope of eternal glories to encircle them, and the welcome of a loving God to embrace them!

The gospel is glorious news for the dying since they may have the welcome of a loving God to embrace them!

Oh, my text is right when it speaks of the glorious gospel. It is an invitation from the most radiant Being who ever walked the earth or ascended the heavens. It is an invitation to you and me to come and be made happy, and then after that to take a royal castle for an everlasting residence, with the angels of God as our cupbearers. *Come unto me, all ye that labour and are heavy laden, and I will give you rest. Take my yoke upon you and learn of me; for I am meek and lowly in heart: and ye shall find rest unto your souls* (Matthew 11:28-29). *Let not your heart be troubled: ye believe in God, believe also in me. In my Father's house are many mansions: if it were not so, I would have told you. I go to prepare a place for you. And if I go and prepare a place for you, I will come again, and receive you unto myself; that where I am, there ye may be also* (John 14:1-3).

THE PRICE OF FORGIVENESS

The price was paid for all of this on the cliff of limestone, which is about seven minutes' walk from the wall of Jerusalem, where with an agony that with one hand tore down the rocks, and with the other drew a midnight blackness over the heavens, our Lord set us forever free. Making no apology for any one of the million sins of our lives, but confessing all of them, we can point to that cliff of limestone and say, "There was paid our indebtedness, and God never collects a bill twice." *There is therefore now no condemnation to them which are in Christ Jesus* (Romans 8:1). *Being now justified by his blood, we shall be saved from wrath through him* (Romans 5:9).

I am glad that all the Christian poets have exerted their pen in praising the matchless One of this gospel.

Isaac Watts, how do you feel about Him?

He writes, "I am not ashamed to own my Lord."

John Newton, what do you think of this gospel?

He writes, "Amazing grace, how sweet the sound!"

William Cowper, what do you think of Him?

The answer comes, "There is a fountain filled with blood."

Charles Wesley, what do you think of Him?

He answers, "Jesus, lover of my soul."

Horatius Bonar, what do you think of Him?

He responds, "I lay my sins on Jesus."

Ray Palmer, what do you think of Him?

He writes, "My faith looks up to Thee."

Fanny Crosby, what do you think of Him?

She writes, "Blessed assurance, Jesus is mine."

However, I take still higher testimony.

Solomon, what do you think of Him?

The answer is: *Lily of the valleys* (Song of Solomon 2:1).

Ezekiel, what do you think of Him?

The answer is: *Plant of renown* (Ezekiel 34:29).

David, what do you think of Him?

He answers: *My shepherd* (Psalm 23:1).

John, what do you think of Him?

The answer is: *Bright and morning star* (Revelation 22:16).

Paul, what do you think of Him?

The answer comes: *Christ is all, and in all* (Colossians 3:11).

O man, O woman, of the blood-bought immortal spirit – do you think the same way of Him? Yes, Paul was right when he called it *the glorious gospel.*

A pharmacist, while you are waiting for him to make up the doctor's prescription, puts into a bottle so many grains of this, and so many grains of that, and so many drops of this, and so many drops of that, and when the mixture is taken, although sour or bitter, it restores to health. In the same way, Christ, the Divine Physician, prepares this trouble of our lifetime, and that disappointment, and this persecution, and that hardship, and that tear, and we must take the mixture, even though it may be bitter, under the divine prescription it administers to our restoration and spiritual health, for all things work together for good (Romans 8:28). Glorious gospel!

Then there is the royal castle into which we step out of this life without so much as soiling our foot with the upturned earth of the grave! *They shall reign for ever and ever* (Revelation 22:5). Does not that mean that if you are saved, you are to be kings and queens – and do not kings and queens have castles? But the One that you are offered was, for thirty-three years, an abandoned castle, though now gloriously inhabited.

There is an abandoned royal castle at Amber, India. One hundred and seventy years ago, a king moved out of it, never to return. But the castle, an indescribable splendor, still stands. You go through bold doorway after bold doorway, and carved room after carved room, and under embellished ceiling after embellished ceiling, and through precious-stoned halls into wider precious-stoned halls. On that hill are pavilions that are deeply dyed, tasseled, and arched. The fire of colored gardens is cooled by the snow of white architecture. There are birds in ornamental work so natural to life that while you cannot hear their voices, you imagine you see the flutter of their wings while you are passing. There are walls pictured with triumphal procession, rooms that were called "Alcove of Light" and "Hall of Victory" that are marble, white and black, like a mixture of morning and night, as well as alabaster and mother-of-pearl and lacquer work.

Standing before this castle, the eye climbs from step to latticed balcony, and from latticed balcony to oriel window, and from oriel window to arch, and from arch to roof, and then descends on ladders of all colors, and by stairs of perfect lines, and on to tropical gardens of pomegranates and pineapples. There are seven stories of resplendent architecture!

But the royal castle provided for you, if you will only take it on the prescribed terms, is grander than all that, and although it was an abandoned castle while Christ was here achieving your redemption, it is again occupied by the *chiefest among ten thousand* (Song of Solomon 5:10), and some of your own kindred who have gone up and are waiting for you are leaning from the balcony. The windows of that castle look out on the King's gardens where immortals walk linked in eternal friendship. The banqueting hall of that castle has princes and princesses at the table. The wine is the new wine of the kingdom (Matthew 26:29), and the supper is the *marriage supper of the Lamb* (Revelation 19:9). There are fountains into which no tear ever fell, and there is music that trembles with no grief. The light that falls upon that scene is never dim, and there is the kiss of those reunited after long separation.

We will have more vigor there than now, or we would faint away under the delight. We will have stronger vision there than now, or our eyesight would be blinded by the brilliance. We will have stronger ears there than now, or under the boom of that singing, the thunder of the hosannas, and the rumble of those hallelujahs, we would be deafened.

Glorious gospel! You thought Christianity was a straitjacket, that it limited you, and that thereafter you must be oppressed. No, no, no! It is to place you in a castle!

By the cleansing power of the shed blood of Golgotha, set your faces toward the shining pinnacles. Oh, it does not matter much what becomes of us here, for at the longest, our stay is short – if we can only end up there. There are so many I do want to meet there: Joshua, my favorite prophet, John among the evangelists, Paul among the apostles, John Wycliffe among the martyrs, Bourdaloue among the preachers, Dante among the poets, Havelock among the heroes, and our loved ones whom we have so much missed since they left us. There are so many dear to the heart, and their absence is sometimes almost unbearable.

Most of all, leaving this for the end because I want the thought utmost in our thoughts, I want to see our blessed Lord, without whom we could never reach the old castle at all. He took our place. He purchased our ransom. He wept our woes. He suffered our stripes. He died our death. He assured our resurrection. Blessed be His glorious name forever! All the anthems will be surging toward His ear! All the honor will be for Him!

Oh, I want to see it, and I will see it – the day of His coronation. He is on a throne already. I think the day will come when in some great hall of eternity, all the nations of earth whom He has conquered by His grace will assemble again to crown Him in the great audience room of heaven – wide and high and immense and adorned as with the sunrises and sunsets of a thousand years. Like the leaves of an Adirondack forest, the ransomed multitudes, with Christ standing on a high place surrounded by worshippers and subjects, will come out of the farthest past led on by the prophets.

They will come out of the early gospel days led on by the apostles. They will come out of the centuries still ahead of us, led on by champions of the truth, heroes and heroines yet to be born.

Then from that vastest audience ever assembled in all the universe, there will go up the shout, "Crown Him! Crown Him! Crown Him!" The Father, who long ago promised this to His only begotten Son (*I shall give thee the heathen for thine inheritance, and the uttermost parts of the earth for thy possession* [Psalm 2:8]), will set the crown upon the forehead still scarred with the crucifixion thorns. All the hosts of heaven, on the ground level and up in the galleries, will drop on their knees crying, "Hail, King of earth! King of heaven! King of saints! King of seraphs! Your kingdom is an everlasting kingdom, and to thy dominions there shall be no end! Amen and Amen! Amen and Amen!"

ETERNITY

I ask you: where will you spend eternity? Oh, prepare for it. Do not put it off until the last hour. Do not wait until you get sick. You may never be sick. Do not leave it until you get more time. You may never get more time. Do not procrastinate until you get old. You may never get old. Do not wait until tomorrow. This night your soul may be required of you (Luke 12:20).

Suppose that in that moment you would say, "Wait until I kneel down and say my prayers." Death would respond, "You do not have time now to say your prayers."

"Wait until I get my friends together and tell them good-bye." Death would say, "You cannot stop to tell them good-bye."

"But I cannot go into eternity with all these sins about me. Give me time to repent." Death would say, "It is too late to repent! Your soul is required of you this hour, this minute, this second!"

Oh, by the cross of Christ, repent! Bow your head this moment and say, *Jesus, thou son of David, have mercy on me* (Luke 18:38). In Christ, you are safe. Out of Him, you perish.

MAN'S QUESTIONS; GOD'S ANSWERS

Am I accountable to God?

Every one of us shall give account of himself to God (Romans 14:12).

Has God seen all my ways?

All things are naked and opened unto the eyes of him with whom we have to do (Hebrews 4:13).

Does He charge me with sin?

The scripture hath concluded all under sin (Galatians 3:22).

All have sinned (Romans 3:23).

Will He punish sin?

The soul that sinneth, it shall die (Ezekiel 18:4).

For the wages of sin is death (Romans 6:23).

Must I perish?

[God is] not willing that any should perish, but that all should come to repentance (2 Peter 3:9).

How can I escape?

Believe on the Lord Jesus Christ, and thou shalt be saved (Acts 16:31).

Is He able to save me?

He is able also to save them to the uttermost that come unto God by him (Hebrews 7:25).

Is He willing?

Christ Jesus came into the world to save sinners (1 Timothy 1:15).

Am I saved when I believe?

He that believeth on the Son hath everlasting life (John 3:36).

Can I be saved now?

Now is the accepted time; behold, now is the day of salvation (2 Corinthians 6:2).

As I am?

Him that cometh to me I will in no wise cast out (John 6:37).

Will I not fall away?

Him that is able to keep you from falling (Jude v. 24).

If saved, how should I live?

They which live should not henceforth live unto themselves, but unto him which died for them (2 Corinthians 5:15).

What about death and eternity?

I go to prepare a place for you; . . . that where I am, there ye may be also (John 14:2-3).

AUTHOR INFORMATION

CHARLES H. SPURGEON (1834-1892)

Charles Haddon Spurgeon was a British Baptist preacher. He started preaching at age sixteen and quickly became famous. He is still known as the "Prince of Preachers," and he frequently had more than ten thousand people present to hear him preach at the Metropolitan Tabernacle in London. His sermons were printed in newspapers, translated into many languages, and published in many books.

J. WILBUR CHAPMAN (1859-1918)

John Wilbur Chapman was an American evangelist, pastor, author, and hymnwriter. He wrote the hymns "One Day" and "Our Great Saviour" (Jesus! What a Friend for sinners!). Chapman became a Christian in his youth, but found assurance of salvation when D. L. Moody personally dealt with him in one of Moody's inquiry rooms. Chapman pastored in Philadelphia and joined B. Fay Mills in some of his evangelistic crusades. He also preached with Moody at the Chicago World's

Fair. Moody called Chapman the greatest evangelist in the country. In addition, Chapman served as vice-president at Moody's Bible institute, hired Billy Sunday when Sunday had just begun preaching, and joined with Sol Dickey to start the Winona Lake Bible Conference.

JOHN MCNEILL (1854-1933)

John McNeill was a Scottish evangelist and pastor. He was called the "Scotch Spurgeon." He moved to London to pastor a church, where he became friends with Charles Spurgeon. D. L. Moody invited McNeill to America, where he preached in evangelistic campaigns. Moody said, "Mr. McNeill is the greatest preacher in the world." McNeill also held evangelistic meetings in other countries, including South Africa, Australia, and India.

B. FAY MILLS (1857-1916)

Benjamin Fay Mills was an American evangelist and pastor. It is estimated that five hundred thousand people were converted to Jesus Christ under his preaching in ten years. He seemed to have started out well, and then wavered for a while in his ministry, exploring other beliefs before returning to Christianity shortly before his death.

DWIGHT L. MOODY (1837-1899)

Dwight Lyman Moody was an American evangelist, chaplain, and Christian worker. He was led to Jesus Christ by his Sunday school teacher, Edward Kimball.

Moody soon left for Chicago and began teaching a Sunday school class of his own. By the time he was twenty-three, he had become a successful shoe sales-man, earning $5,000 in only eight months. Having decided to follow Jesus, though, he left his career to engage in Christian work for only $300 a year. He was a chaplain during the Civil War, started schools for both boys and girls, and helped start the Chicago Evangelization Society (now Moody Bible Institute). It is estimated that during his lifetime, Moody traveled more than one million miles, preached to more than one million people, and personally dealt with more than seven hundred and fifty thousand individuals.

T. DE WITT TALMAGE (1832-1902)

Thomas De Witt Talmage was an American pastor, author, and reformer. He is probably best known for pastoring the Brooklyn Tabernacle in New York. The church burned down three times during his twenty-five years there. He later pastored in Washington, D.C. He was also a chap-lain during the Civil War and led crusades against sin and crime. His sermons were published weekly in more than three thousand newspapers, and it is estimated that thirty thousand people were saved under his ministry. Charles Spurgeon said, "Mr. Talmage's discourses lay hold of my inmost soul. The Lord is with this mighty man of valor. So may he ever be till the campaign closes with victory! I am indeed glad of his voice. It cheers me intensely. He loves the gospel, and believes in something, which some preachers hardly do."

OTHER SIMILAR TITLES

Jesus Came to Save Sinners,
by Charles H. Spurgeon

This is a heart-level conversation with you, the reader. Every excuse, reason, and roadblock for not coming to Christ is examined and duly dealt with. If you think you may be too bad, or if perhaps you really are bad and you sin either openly or behind closed doors, you will discover that life in Christ is for you too. You can reject the message of salvation by faith, or you can choose to live a life of sin after professing faith in Christ, but you cannot change the truth as it is, either for yourself or for others. As such, it behooves you and your family to embrace truth, claim it for your own, and be genuinely set free for now and eternity. Come and embrace this free gift of God, and live a victorious life for Him.

Available where books are sold.

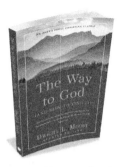

The Way to God
by Dwight L. Moody

There is life in Christ. Rich, joyous, wonderful life. It is true that the Lord disciplines those whom He loves and that we are often tempted by the world and our enemy, the devil. But if we know how to go beyond that temptation to cling to the cross of Jesus Christ and keep our eyes on our Lord, our reward both here on earth and in heaven will be 100 times better than what this world has to offer.

This book is thorough. It brings to life the love of God, examines the state of the unsaved individual's soul, and analyzes what took place on the cross for our sins. *The Way to God* takes an honest look at our need to repent and follow Jesus, and gives hope for unending, joyous eternity in heaven.

Available where books are sold.

Printed in Great Britain
by Amazon